DREAM ALOUD!

ADJUST YOUR LIFESTYLE AND LIVELIHOOD TO MATCH YOUR DESIRES

KENDRA NEWMAN

Copyright © 2024

ALL RIGHTS RESERVED.
Published in the United States by Pen Legacy Publishing
An imprint of Pen Legacy, LLC, Pennsylvania
www.penlegacy.com

Library of Congress Cataloging–in–Publication Data has been applied for.

Paperback ISBN:979-8-9918247-5-0

PRINTED IN THE UNITED STATES OF AMERICA.

FIRST EDITION

TABLE OF CONTENTS

Preface	7
About This Book	9
Who Inspires You?	19
Who Were You Meant to Be in The First Place?	29
My Adjusted Lifestyle and Livelihood	39
What Do You Believe?	55
How Do You See Yourself?	67
Designing A Life and Livelihood of Impact with The 3L Jumpoff Methodology	99
The Pivot and Parlay Process	111
Signs That You Need to Create Your Exit Strategy Now	129
Hush Your Inner Critic	159
If You Don't Know Where You're Going, Any Road Will Get You There	165
Retreatment	179
5 Keys to Live Your Dreams	183
About The Author	205

DREAM ALOUD

**ADJUST YOUR LIFESTYLE & LIVELIHOOD
TO MATCH YOUR DESIRES**

Preface

If your approach to having what you want means being gainfully employed at any cost so that you can enjoy the life it affords you outside of work, then I say this with love...you may be doing it wrong. You see, you CAN do it the old way—working hard and enjoying yourself when you have time off, but old ways of tap dancing for pay and benefits won't deliver new results. Society will make you believe you need to wear masks, play the game, and tap dance your way to the corner office to have the life of your dreams. While that may have been true (or a common belief) in the past, I'm here to tell you that the old approach to transforming your lifestyle may address most material desires, but it sucks the soul dry.

The reasons my clients love the *Lifestyle Over Livelihood* approach are simple:

- They gain clarity, courage, and confidence to pursue the life they truly want.
- It's a roadmap for building a solid foundation so they can effortlessly transition into their soul-satisfying second, third, or eightieth act without losing their shirts.
- They walk away with a tried-and-true strategy to create new income doing what they love, allowing them to be more fulfilled with less regret.

So why would you keep doing things the old way? My *Dream Aloud!* approach to living as you desire will accelerate your transition from merely having financial safety to a fulfilled mind, body, lifestyle, bank account, business, and, ultimately, a legacy worthy of talking about. Sounds like a no-brainer to me. If you agree, keep reading.

About This Book

What makes your heart sing? When did you first do that thing that made you light up inside? How did you feel? How often do you do it?

Whew! That battery of questions may have caught you off guard, but it's my way of engaging your curiosity, which helps when deciding on your best next big thing. If you answered, "I don't do it anymore," or "I have no idea what makes my heart sing," then you have chosen the right book to figure it out so you can get on track to living life passionately on purpose. Whether you are just beginning a career, winding down to retirement, starting a side hustle, or stepping full-time into your own business, you should always ask yourself what's next and what it will take to get there—while living the best life possible, of course. The best life possible includes living the lifestyle that brings you the most peace and joy while doing what you love, or, in other words, doing the things that make your heart sing.

Kendra Newman

Are you wondering what's next for you or how to get where you want to be? May I suggest that you first decide what you will do to figure out what you want and create a roadmap to get there?

I can hear your thoughts... No, you don't have to create every detail of the roadmap, but you need to start doing new things and learning what you like and don't like. Yes, even those of you who are seasoned experts need to try new things to help set yourselves on the next trajectory of the dreams you have. Let's face it, what we thought we wanted at age eighteen is probably not exactly what we wish to have at thirty. Our desires will continue to change as we evolve through the years, and the best way to handle constant change is to embrace it. When we are willing to pivot with the times and circumstances of life, we'll find solutions, new desires, and unsolicited opportunities.

Embrace that your roadmap will have a desired end that may change a little—or a great deal—as you go about your journey. You have the right to change that end as you and your view of life shift through experience. In high school and college, I dreamed of having a huge house with land, a high-powered position that paid well, traveling the world, and helping my family financially with my real estate investment profits. However, at thirty-five, I gladly put my unpresumptuous 1,200-square-foot home up for sale after eight years of ownership. The monetary gain from the sale was nice, but that's not all. It lifted my burden of maintaining the property and paying municipal taxes. Also, the fact that I only used three rooms in my home made me realize that my dream of owning a huge house was no longer my desire. As a single mom with a teen, I was preparing to live for me. With the sale of my house, I had fewer responsibilities and more money to travel while making moves to qualify for higher-paying positions after completing my master's degree.

Dream Aloud!

Three years later, I was in the power position of my dreams, which unfortunately turned into a nightmare. After seven years of successes on a rocky road in a toxic work environment and lessons learned, I pivoted to working for myself to give myself better income choices while still being employed by an organization.

While I'm now with an employer that offers a much better environment for work-life balance, I have put in place a heart-centered business and secured other streams of income that help me live my jubilee decade freer than I ever imagined during my seven years in "Dream Job" hell. It's not perfect, but how many things in life usually are? However, the lifestyle-aligned livelihood I've created for myself while doing the things I love provides supplemental income. This additional income means I won't have to put myself on spending restrictions due to a fixed income during my retirement. Spending freedom, good health, traveling, sharing my story to help others, and having a little wealth to pass on for posterity are my dreams now.

Here's a story for you:

Standing at the podium, I told my story of being a single mom of one young adult son who had gone to college with me before he went to kindergarten. Determined not to be a statistic, I took my responsibility as a mother seriously. My parents offered their support by watching my son during the week while I was away at school, but I would come home every weekend to be a mommy. I had seen what happened when young parents left their child(ren) to be raised by someone else, usually the child(ren)'s grandparent or great-grandparent. The result was often resentment and a strained relationship between the parent and child(ren). I decided to take that as a lesson and embody the role of mommy in my son's life. I remembered Chris Rock's line from one of his

Kendra Newman

standup routines: *"If the kid calls his grandmama 'Momma' and his mama 'Pam', he's goin' to jail."* I had plenty of real-life examples to believe this statement was a truth I did not want to experience.

Michael Clemens, Associate Director of Workforce Development, and I headed over to the university lecture hall about one hour after he asked me to speak to a group of community members who were being prepared to become employees of the higher education institution in the center of their neighborhood if they chose to do so. Michael Robinson, Director of Community Outreach and Hiring, created and ran the program. After we were introduced, Mr. Robinson teased me with a hint of seriousness that I needed to bring down the house, to which I replied that I always close when I take the mic. That wasn't true every single time I stood before an audience. However, it was the truth whenever I told my story of going from being a single mother on welfare to Director of Technology & Information Management for a college with seven individual units over three campuses and various off-campus clinics and centers.

I shared with the participants the pursuit of my dreams to support myself and my son by doing something I loved that would complement my life and lifestyle. I knew I needed a career that would not require me to work overtime, weekends, or holidays. I also wanted a job with plenty of family time, travel, and, most importantly, minimal stress so that work issues would not overshadow my time with my son. My audience had many questions about how I became a technology and project management expert and what it takes to earn the Project Management Professional (PMP) credential I used to set myself apart from other candidates in the Higher Ed Technology Management space. I went into detail about taking advantage of

Dream Aloud!

every opportunity to gain experience that would provide me with a diverse background and a unique skill set. One of my opportunities included attending a technical school that offered hands-on labs because I didn't have time to go to classes at a college or university, work an internship, and take care of my four-year-old, who began living with me full-time after my mother's death.

There are no words to explain the feeling I had when I left the building more than two hours later. While walking me out, both Michaels expressed how they were thoroughly impressed with my presentation, but no one was more satisfied than me. I felt this way whenever I stood before people and poured out information that would help them learn something new to improve their lives. The feeling would rise within me each time I presented my thesis in class and later, after graduation, when I began teaching technology for the organizations where I had worked or volunteered.

In 2005, I hosted my first family reunion in Chicago and was the keynote speaker. Family members thanked me for the fun, engaging, and unique banquet that taught them much about their history. The satisfaction I experienced let me know this was what I was supposed to do, but how does one get paid the money needed to travel the world speaking and hosting experiential learning events? It was clear I loved to tell my story and teach through story. The impact on my life and the lives of others was immediate for me and my audience. I then began teaching technology and project management as an adjunct, leading me to the world of people management, diversity, and inclusion. I simply teach what I know through coaching, conferences, and retreats. It's what I was born to do. I'm naturally an encourager with a keen way of teaching by facilitating experiences conducive

13

to learning and impact. In addition to storytelling, my gifts include helping others, seeing the talents and purpose in others before they do, and putting together a plan to make what they were born to do a reality. Before I had a name for it, I was doing this.

Did you recognize the pattern? What's the pattern in your life? Even if you cannot answer this question now, we'll go through some exercises at the end of each chapter to help you create your plan for your next big thing upon completing this book.

I've been leveraging the skills I have acquired along my life's journey to support the lifestyle I've dreamed of living. While most of my ventures have been successful, quite a few have put me in financial binds, knocked my confidence, and caused me to entertain the thought of quitting on several occasions. The beauty of these troubles is that there is always a lesson to be learned in hard times. Even more importantly, none of the lessons have to be wasted; they can be used to improve your circumstances.

As I near retirement, my goal is to teach others what I know about living a full, purposeful life and setting a mark of success that's meaningful to oneself. Society will try to tell us what success should be: money, a big house, a power-matching spouse, two kids, a dog, degrees and titles, and jet-setting worldwide without a care, etc. There are plenty of people who have followed the societal recipe, only to find that they are unhappy and unfulfilled, as well as spiritually, mentally, and often physically poor. To avoid or pull yourself out of this trap, you must define your ideal life and set your own parameters for success. Then, you'll be ready to create a livelihood that fits your lifestyle, not vice versa. We were meant to live our best, unique lives that also make the world a better place. Unfortunately, too many have subscribed to a "best life" defined by Hollywood and world

Dream Aloud!

media. Our environment and social norms shape our opinions of what is acceptable, and so much of what we believe was taught without a single formal lesson. In order to step into our rightful purpose and live our dreams, we must make some changes. The decision to change also requires action, a shift in thinking, and the audacity to believe that the dreams in our hearts have been placed there for us to live them OUT LOUD AND IN COLOR!

We experience life in many ways, learning our likes and dislikes along the way. As a student of life and an experienced people-watcher, I have put together a collection of thoughts and action items to help you discover your next direction in life and create a livelihood that supports the lifestyle of your dreams. Keep in mind that a dream was placed in your heart so you can pursue it. Also, make sure you understand that you can have more than one dream; you don't have to pick just one! Don't limit yourself. While I recommend that you have a strategy for prioritizing which goals or dreams to accomplish first, remember it's not just a choice of *which* dream you will pursue, but knowing you are worthy of *"both AND"* instead of *"either-or."* Each dream in your heart has been placed there to be fulfilled. Accept the assignment and go for it.

Your dreams are uniquely yours, but not just for your benefit. We are all connected, and when you answer the call to fulfill your purpose, you empower others to answer theirs. Think about those who have answered their call and how it has affected you. How could you even be in the space that you are now if you hadn't had some examples of the life you wanted? How could you want more from life if you hadn't seen more than you could imagine from others? If you're going to live life beyond the status quo, please promise you'll begin today to dance like nobody's watching. I can assure you, however, that the right people are indeed watching. You may never know their names, but that's not important. Your life should speak volumes to the people in your sphere of influence.

If you don't do it, they'll have to wait for someone braver than you, with a similar calling, to act. Don't let them or yourself down. ACT NOW, and watch doors begin to open. Remember, nothing will happen until you move. It is then that the universe will be signaled to support your efforts. You'll find that the things you need but don't have in your possession will begin manifesting in many forms to assist your progress. Don't believe me? Try it. The moment you're busy doing what's necessary to get ahead, people and opportunities will show up with exactly what you need.

Here's an example:

I started my business during the pandemic (an opportunity to prove my theory that my job could be done without going into the office), and most of my interactions with clients and partners were online. As the shelter-in-place order lifted, I was able to go out and speak in public. Then, my father became ill, and I suspended all my events to spend time with him. After four months of hospice care, my dad passed, and during my time of deep mourning, I did almost nothing for my business—just focused on catching up on the work I did for my employer. In April 2024, I decided I wanted to begin speaking again. The very people I had planned to reach out to in hopes of being their Juneteenth speaker contacted me to ask me to be a keynote speaker for their women's program, and this happened only four hours after I had decided to take action.

I had only five days to prepare, but their theme was on point with a topic I spoke on, so I was ready. Not only was I able to bring a strong message—letting the ladies know they have a

Dream Aloud!

duty to seize their birthright, control how their story is told, and that their legacy depends on it—but I also got the push I needed to return to public speaking, something I had desired to do seven weeks before Juneteenth.

This goes for you, too. Remember, you are entitled to your birthright by the mere fact of being born. Most importantly, it's yours for the taking as long as you don't believe you'll have a hard time getting what's due to you. If an opportunity to do what you love falls into your lap, take it!

If you were able to see the lesson in my story, you now know that sometimes the only thing you need to do is DECIDE you want something, and it can happen before you make a move. In other cases, being definitive is not enough, and you must DO something before what you want comes to you. There will also be times when you'll have to fight for what's due to you, but always remember it's still yours.

If you couldn't already tell, I'm a storyteller, and this book is full of stories. So, brace yourself for this style of impartation. Following the stories, you will be prompted to take action. After all, nothing will work until you do. Lastly, feel free to drop me a line at connectwithkendra.com to schedule a quick chat to discuss anything about this book.

Kendra Newman

ACTION ITEMS:

1. Get a notebook or journal to take notes as you read through each chapter and record the activities you've completed under each Action Items section. Be sure to include how you FEEL about the chapter, the completed action items, and your lessons learned.
2. Think back to the things you do for fun, whether as a hobby or something you naturally do. What's the pattern? Do friends, family, and colleagues call on you because you're the best person they know to accomplish what needs to be done?
3. Ask others what you do best. For example, ask them which three of your talents they would use if you were working for them.
4. Moving forward, when you decide to do something, take note of what happens. Did what you wanted or needed to happen show up serendipitously, or was there a waiting period?

Who Inspires You?

I have interviewed phenomenal women (and men) who dared to pivot from what they believed to be the best circumstances for their lives to pursue their lifelong or new dreams instead. Some kept those dreams a secret, fearing others would think they were crazy to give up so much to go after something that might seem far-fetched. My interviewees have had a dream call (in some cases repeatedly) and finally decided they were no longer willing to ignore it. They found themselves needing to bet on themselves. It's the only way not to be haunted by the "what ifs" in the end. My podcasts are full of the "Shoulda, Woulda, Coulda Club" (which we'll discuss later) membership-resistant folks. These selected guests have done what many aspire to, and they are examples of what happens when someone would rather try and fail than wonder what could have been if they had only tried. In most of my interviews, I've learned that ninety percent of those who dare to pivot and "fail" find something better (a new way of doing what they wanted, a different path, etc.) than they initially set out to do.

My podcast takes on a conversation-style type of interviewing and typically lasts about thirty minutes. However, some run well past the half-hour mark because we stream live on social media and answer questions from those tuning in. We want to lend ourselves to inspiration instead of being fixated on sticking to a schedule. Depending on the vibe, these interviews could have multiple parts when added to my YouTube channel. (Search "Kendra Newman" for my YouTube channel. Then subscribe, like, and share. Thank you in advance.)

At the end of every episode, I ask two questions: *What's your favorite quote?* and *On whose shoulders do you stand?* I love quotes, especially those from elders, because they are life experiences left to guide us when we encounter something new. It's like having a guiding light from others who have traveled a similar path to the one we are currently traversing. None of us gets anywhere in life without the support and sacrifice of others, and so I believe it is important to recognize the people who've gone before us. They are the reason we occupy spaces that they or their parents could only dream of holding. When we speak the names of those who have made it possible for us to occupy the spaces we do, they forever live in our hearts from generation to generation.

Maya Angelou is the best example of how one woman answering her life's calling has inspired countless others, including me. I was twenty-two years old when her books began to speak to me. My mother had recently passed away, and I felt abandoned by her (although I know getting cancer and dying were not her choice) and by my three-year-old son's father. The two of them had insisted that I not abort my pregnancy, which

Dream Aloud!

threatened my dreams of going to college and making more money so I could travel the world. I never really considered being married or having children before I found myself eighteen and pregnant. One year later, I was engaged to someone with whom I had no desire to unite with in matrimony. However, I dreamed of owning a lavish house I designed, traveling the world, and enjoying the company of a man who loved me. Now, here I was, a single mother with a little boy whom I loved but who was a great responsibility. My dad was a big help but didn't promise to assist me in the same capacity as my mom. Three years into the deal, she was no longer with us, and my baby's daddy was long gone once he realized he couldn't hold me hostage in an abusive relationship or stop me from leaving for college with a child.

I decided to shift my dreams to include one of the best blessings God can grant us—a child. From that day on, my son's life became part of my dream lifestyle, and fortunately, I had plenty of examples of single mothers who lived full lives while making a way for themselves and their children. My grandmothers and Maya Angelou were my examples. Let's focus on Dr. Angelou. She was also a teen mom, but that didn't stop her from pursuing her life's dream. She became the first Black woman streetcar conductor in San Francisco because she was told she couldn't be. Before she became a professor, writer, and poet, she ran a brothel after prostituting at another. She was also a cook, dancer, and actress and learned to speak several languages during her travels through Europe and Africa. What I loved most about Mother Maya was her allowing herself to experience life on her terms. Regardless of what society said she should be, she marched to the beat of her own drum, doing what made her heart sing.

Kendra Newman

All of this is good, but I'm not Dr. Angelou. I am me, and there is no one else like me. That goes for you, too. Don't let those who inspired you create your path. Now is the time to be honest with yourself. Have you chosen a career path because someone else made it look easy or suggested that you do it? How has that worked out for you? Just because you can do a job, or even do it well, doesn't mean you should. Whether you've selected a path in line with your purpose and passion, creating a livelihood you love, or you find yourself in a work environment that looks good but doesn't make you feel good, there's always room for improvement and change.

Our lives have seasons, and while our purpose stays the same, our assignments change. Let's say Amy's purpose is to improve everything she touches. How does she know that's her purpose? Because she continually walks into spaces and finds ways to make things better. She turns good things into great things and makes what's not so good acceptable. She's the one who upgrades everything. When she was six, she rearranged the Thanksgiving setting of the kids' table, which made the adults envious. She's the go-to person for beautifying all things, especially parties and weddings.

When asked if she would do this for a living, she says she cannot. She likes being an executive assistant. It pays well, and she gets to travel alongside her boss, Laura, the highest-ranking female executive at the Fortune 500 company. Amy loves making her look good and having her ear to help raise the consciousness of young girls and women. Anytime Laura is available, Amy doesn't hesitate to book her for fundraisers, fireside chats, and one-on-one interviews with individuals looking to explore leadership roles. Sometimes, the company will host events with Laura billed as the keynote speaker, and

Dream Aloud!

Amy plans everything from the menu, décor, and program order.

Now I ask again: What is the pattern here? Not only is it obvious that Amy is good at making things beautiful and better, but she is also trusted by many to make things happen for others. Maybe because these things come naturally to her, she doesn't see them as a big deal and brushes them off as something she simply does. Please note that whatever comes easily to you is usually not so easy for others. That, my friend, is where your compensation lies. The demand for Amy to create enticing spaces, along with her influence and connection to highly sought-after figures, did not just start with her employment at a Fortune 500 company; she has been influencing others (including her elders) since she was at least six years old.

Suppose we dive into Amy's life from age six to now. We would probably see her delegating connections among students and teachers in grade school, serving on the prom committee in high school, and being the reason the centerpieces at her cousin's wedding were the talk of the town. I'll point out patterns as we go through this book. Your job is to analyze and determine the person's gifts, talents, and skills. First, we need to understand the differences between each.

A **gift** is something you're born with but cannot take credit for, such as your height, looks, creativity, or photographic memory. Your **talent** shows up in the form of what you are good at doing and, with practice and nurturing, can become better. In some cases, you may even be exceptional compared to others. **Skill** is what you've been trained to do: cooking, plumbing, carpentry, computer programming, etc. It's easy to confuse these three things (gift, talent, skill) because we often start with one and end up with the others. For example, Amy is creatively gifted and has used her gift to become a talented decorator. Now, she has taken the advice of her friends and family and enrolled in courses to become a skilled interior designer.

Jealousy often indicates what you may want or need to pursue. I call it inspiration in reverse. It is a natural emotion that must be managed. Whenever you feel a twinge of envy because someone does something you'd like to do or gets results you'd like to have, ask yourself what that feeling is trying to tell you. Are you feeling like they have something you don't and will never have? Then ask yourself if that's really true.

Think about the co-worker who seems to be "failing up". Let's say, for example, I was on tour with Maya Angelou and her castmates from Porgy and Bess as they traveled through Europe and Africa. I can imagine being one of the castmates jealous that she spoke seven languages and was invited to dinner parties in the private homes of residents in multiple countries. One might imagine she received better treatment and had a better experience than me.

The minute I feel resentment for her treatment, I have to acknowledge that feeling. Once acknowledged, I should ask myself why I resent her: *She was invited by others.* Is it her fault I cannot speak fluently at their dinner table, or am I just too shy to speak the little German I know? Is it true that the hosts cannot speak English or would be unwilling to do so if I were their guest?

What lies have I told myself to get to this feeling of being lesser than others? Unless I had asked Maya Angelou who invited her and knew the conversation, I would've had to make up the parts of the story I didn't know. When I fill in the blanks with what I think the story is, I fall for my ideas of what happened based on my experience and not necessarily the truth. I could hate her for speaking seven languages and thus having more freedom in other countries, or I could ask her how she

Dream Aloud!

learned them. Once I have the information from the source (not the lies I tell myself), I can decide if I want to speak other languages. Do I wish to put in the time to learn? Will I practice? And once I have a foundational vocabulary, will I dare to put myself out there to engage in dialogue with native speakers?

Whenever you feel tempted to envy someone for what they have, I suggest you think about what makes you want it, too. Next, take the time to figure out why you feel that you cannot have it, and then ask yourself if that is true. Much of the time, the answer is not that you cannot have what they have; the answer is more about your willingness to do what they did to get it.

Pay attention to who and what inspires you. When you find yourself inspired by someone, ask yourself what you admire most about them. By doing so, you'll find clues to what you like to do and what you're passionate about. Trying new things will help you add more to your list of likes and even recognize your dislikes. Making time to do more of what you enjoy will reveal your passion. Our passion is generally tied to our purpose. Please note that some passions we have may be part of our assignment to just support someone else. I love justice and community but am not called to run for office. My assignment is to support those who educate and run for local political offices.

TIP: It is important not only to be willing to do and have what you like, but you also have to be able to. While I am fascinated by languages and like that Maya Angelou spoke seven, it doesn't mean I'm cut out to be an interpreter. More likely, I'm drawn to her ability to harness her multiple talents and create streams of income while living a fulfilled life. Like Maya, I was born with the gift of storytelling and improved my talent through writing and speaking naturally. I've become a skilled presenter who routinely gets on stage in front of classrooms to teach what I know, using examples that include stories. Storytelling is part of my life's work, and I've been doing it since before entering elementary school.

Your job is what you've been trained to do, but your work is what you were born to do. The best situation is having a job that aligns with your work. Finding a job that aligns with your life's work may not always be possible, but you can always create one.

Dream Aloud!

ACTION ITEMS:

Find a quiet place, let your mind settle, and then ask your heart, "Who do I admire?"

_____
_____
_____
_____
_____
_____
_____

Now ask yourself, "What are the qualities of the person (or people) that make me admire them?"

_____
_____
_____
_____
_____
_____
_____
_____
_____

Kendra Newman

Hold on to this list. We'll use it as you continue reading. List anything that stands out to you after completing your list in your journal.

Has a particular thought or question raised interest or investigations since you've made this list? If so, share below.

_____
_____
_____
_____
_____
_____
_____
_____
_____
_____
_____
_____
_____
_____
_____

Who Were You Meant to Be in The First Place?

"Maybe the journey is not to become anything. Maybe it's to undo all of the things that are not you so you can be who you were meant to be in the first place."

This quote appeared on my social media page back in 2020, and it summed up everything I was going through during the pandemic. I asked myself, *Is this my opportunity to live on an even higher level of purpose?* Prior to the COVID shelter-in-place rules, I asked myself, *Is this all life has to offer?*

I'd made it through, as the church people say. Pre-COVID, my life was filled with setting goals and achieving them. I had raised my child and embarked on the future of freedom I had looked forward to once he graduated from high school. For the most part, keeping my dreams in sight is what keeps me motivated.

Kendra Newman

I had fulfilled most of my life goals: college graduation, getting a good job, buying a house, earning a master's degree without incurring more student loan debt, assuming a leadership position in higher education, raising a good person, getting married, and continuing to travel the world. The last two were borderline accomplishments, but I'd checked each off my bucket list. Not every accomplishment was easy. There had been plenty of sleepless nights and opportunities to quit that I considered more than twice. Then, I got comfortable. Family and friends would comment, "You've done so much. What more do you want to do?" and "I wish I'd been as focused as you." These and similar comments made me feel like reaching for anything else would be overkill. So, I began to settle into my good-enough life. It was a life that other people wanted and one that I enjoyed, but I kept feeling there was more life to experience.

March 2020's shelter-in-place order allowed me to explore a life I thought I wanted. For over a decade, before the pandemic hit, I wondered what it would be like to work from home. When the U.S. was hit hardest by the virus, I took advantage of the opportunity to explore what had formerly been my commute time to write a book, start my coaching business, and be coached in both areas by experts who had been where I wanted to go. By the time three years had passed, I had experienced some successes and many losses. There were lessons learned from both outcomes. The greatest lesson was the ability to authentically feel soul satisfaction. I knew I was built for a work-from-anywhere lifestyle. Writing my book and being invited to speak in various places about life, especially my culture of formerly enslaved African descendants, reinforced that I am a crafty storyteller with a gift for weaving information and imparting

Dream Aloud!

lessons to help others be their authentic selves and live, work, and play on their terms.

The moment we start doing what we love in a manner that also generates income, we begin to walk in our purpose with passion and build the lifestyle we were created to live. We are born for a purpose and arrive on our day of birth eager to complete our assignment. Then life happens. We're raised with the beliefs and fears of our guardians at home, in our schools, communities, and countries. This rearing, along with our own life experiences, builds our personal belief system filled with mantras that we hold true. When we let go of what others want for us and begin to undo the things placed upon us, we can truly understand the journey. Everything we go through from the moment we set our intention to live a full life as purposed at birth is meant to rid ourselves of everything that isn't truly us.

Let me share proof that life keeps showing us who we really are: My college roommates and I sat around the kitchen table, giggling, talking, and laughing into the wee hours of the morning. My 22-year-old self said, "I thought when I was grown, I'd be so serious, and here we are acting like little kids." Everyone agreed we had an impression of adulthood that doesn't truly exist. That day, we decided to accept that the kid inside would show up on many occasions and that we should welcome her because it felt good. I've learned over the years that while the body has changed and the mind has matured, I am the same person at my core, with more experience and a different—probably more limited—perspective than when I began my best life journey. You are who you are, and your personality is set. I now know that children are not possessions or clones of their parents. They are their OWN SELVES, little individuals—people with personal preferences, likes, and dislikes.

Kendra Newman

Now ask yourself, is how you make a living aligned with who you truly are? Usually, when asked who we are, we tend to respond with what we do for a living and who we are in relationship to others (daughter, mother, sister, friend, co-worker, etc.) But who are you at your core? When we can answer that question matter-of-factly, we are no longer confused about what we should do for a living, the legacy we want to create, and the lifestyle that best suits us. Often, we choose careers and spouses because we think the life that these decisions will provide is what we want. Is it really, though? Are we choosing for the right reasons?

We only need to go back to the little girl inside. Ask her who you were born to be and your life's assignments. She's clear on the details and waiting to be consulted. Get quiet and remember who she was before life happened—before well-meaning parents and teachers (in school and the community) told her how she was expected to act, think, and be. Ask her what she would have been or done if those interferences had not been encountered. Write them down and think of ways to get back to your original purpose with that little girl as your guide.

My friend Keywanda has always received compliments from people everywhere for her creativity— from wearing her grandmother's lampshade crystals as earrings to turning dollar store vases into exotic glassware for her table settings. Her greatest claim to fame was doing the hair of her college colleagues in her apartment kitchen, which became known as Key's Kitchen. The person would arrive for a perm, cut, and style--often done for free—and leave with a hairdo that rivaled those done at local salons and seen in magazines. Best of all was her weave work, now known as hair extensions. I would get so many compliments on my hair that I would proudly tell them it was a weave and that Keywanda did it.

Dream Aloud!

One day, I accompanied her to a neighborhood salon to get her eyebrows arched. While I waited in the sitting area for her, the salon owner commented that my hair was beautiful. I thanked him and told him that it was a weave. His expression was priceless, and with a smirk, he replied, "I know a weave when I see one. You need to stop playing." I then invited him to touch my glued-in tracks. (Keep in mind it was the 1990s, and college students didn't have time for sew-ins back then.) He immediately offered Keywanda the opportunity to work in his salon under his apprenticeship program so she could get her cosmetology license and provide his customers with great styles.

At the time, my friend was working at a nursing home as a receptionist (mainly for health benefits) and going to school for accounting. Although she wanted to take the salon owner up on his offer, she had been taught that she needed a stable, steady-paying job with benefits to be successful. Accounting was her second career path, and she was good at it. Her dream was to be a businesswoman with a staff and a corner office overlooking the Hudson River. She never spoke of working her way up the corporate ladder or owning her own firm. She did express her desire to be featured wearing all white on the covers of *Forbes*, *Ebony*, *Essence*, and *Black Enterprise*.

Seven years later, she was a military wife who had married her college sweetheart, was under the age of thirty, had two kids, and was still pursuing her accounting degree after countless starts and stops. For over a decade, I kept telling her that she needed to become a professional hairstylist and even open her own salon. Yet, she was convinced that an accounting degree and a 9-to-5 job in bean counting were her ticket to a great future for herself and her family. Her parents thought so, too, and her husband was on board. For her, accounting was her way of meeting societal standards of stability. While it was a noble career, it was not her calling. Therefore, what would have looked like success to others would have left her feeling unfulfilled and wondering if it was what she truly wanted for her life.

Fast forward to today. Keywanda has been a salon owner and employer to many for over twenty-five years. In addition, she has a beauty business academy, a skin and hair care line, and a perfume line in the works as I'm writing this. Her business acumen has also led her to create new streams of income, such as her better-than-eggnog anytime drink, Bednog. Now, imagine if she had continued to ignore her talents and desires, choosing not to push against norms. We wouldn't know the lady with the platinum hair as the beauty broker who helps others in the business find their lane. There would probably be no Bednog for us to enjoy, and she would have no story to inspire others to follow their dreams. Those interested in learning more about Keywanda and what she offers can find her online at kavaskincare.com and bednog.com.

Looking back over my life, I've come full circle to who I authentically am on many occasions. I'm a rule follower, so I tend to follow the instructor's steps and then tweak the lessons taught to fit my personality. At my core, I am an experiential teacher who encourages others. I impart what I know to others through heartfelt storytelling, whether in the classroom, on social media, on stage, or during one-on-one coaching sessions. I love studying people and probably know before they do what their next profitable move should be in alignment with their purpose. When I tell them what I believe they should do for a living, it's often in combination with some talent they give away for free. There is frequent resistance because it requires them to put themselves and their dreams first, and they're unsure if a

Dream Aloud!

new path will suit them. What if they fail? What if it doesn't work out? What about everyone else who needs them? Their lives are pretty good. However, they have an inkling it could be so much more. But how? If you have these questions swirling around in your head, it is probably your inner core—the person who you indeed are and were born to be—nudging you because it knows you were made for more! Now you must decide whether you will pursue what you want or settle for good enough.

Think of the things you always do—and do well. You'll find a pattern of doing at least one of those things naturally, and please don't concern yourself with how "small" you might think it is. Remember, we're throwing societal norms out the window. What society considers small could be your gift to create the lifestyle, legacy, and livelihood of your dreams and possibly someone else's dreams.

I've always been a helper, problem solver, and solution creator. It's no wonder I'm a technology and project management expert. My heart is for people. Therefore, my focus—even in an organization where I am classified as a W-2 employee—is to help stakeholders understand how to utilize tech to make their work processes more effective and efficient, along with assisting them in building a plan to implement it in their daily work practices.

My coaching clients come to me to figure out what's next for their lives. We start by building a big picture of their life dreams and then break them down into small tasks to accomplish over a period of time until their dreams become a reality. That way, when they are ready to transition into their next big thing (retirement, a new career, entrepreneurship, etc.), they do so with confidence, having tweaked and tested their new endeavors

Kendra Newman

while ensuring they're aligned with their purpose and passion. Another aspect of what I do and love is planning and managing luxury destination retreats for busy experts who wish to host impactful bucket-list getaways for their clients to get the most out of their retreat experience. The hosts need only show up and impart their expertise as promised to their participants. My team and I handle the logistics, allowing the hosts to take the rest they deserve and enjoy the event with the attendees.

Initially, my lifestyle and livelihood plan as an 18-year-old included pursuing an electrical engineering degree. I could do the work, but it didn't excite me. I didn't want to be in a lab with other geeks. (Yes, I'm a proud geek who likes to hang out with diverse groups.) I wanted to be out in the industry, watching trends, helping people adjust to the changes that technology brings, and studying how to manage change. Truthfully, I'm only fully satisfied when doing what I was created to do. I've always come full circle while trying many things throughout my life. I know that I will not like everything I try, and even the things I like may not be part of my purpose or goals at the time. Whenever I feel a sense of accomplishment in my core and ask myself how I can experience more of this feeling, that's when I tap into discovering more of what I was created to do. It's my job to undo what is not truly me and make it so.

While I was writing this book, a box of Oprah's daily inspirational note cards arrived in the mail. The card on top, still in the shrink wrap, read as follows:

We're only ever being led back home to ourselves. And that ultimately all of this is happening for us to realize who we are at the deepest level.

~ Panache Desai

Dream Aloud!

Now I ask you, who are you really, and what do you need to undo, unravel, and unbelieve to be YOU fully at your deepest level?

Remember my experiences speaking to aspiring university staff from the community, organizing my first family reunion, teaching what I know as an adjunct, and the satisfaction I received from doing all these things? Think back to a time when you felt in your inner core that what you were doing was in line with your purpose.

ACTION ITEMS:

Write down what you did and how it made you feel. Don't wait to do this later. NOW is the time to act.

_____
_____
_____
_____
_____
_____
_____
_____

Now, think of other times when you felt the same way. What strikes a chord with you every time?

_____
_____
_____
_____
_____
_____
_____
_____

My Adjusted Lifestyle and Livelihood

Today, I spend my life preparing for retirement while still working full-time. My job requires me to work ten hours or less daily, Monday through Friday. I'm getting paid to do what I love, and I can do it with my eyes closed in an environment that makes it easy to show up for work. This leaves me four hours daily to work on my businesses and build passive income streams. In less than a decade, I'll be retired and still vibrant. The key is to live for today and plan for the future. Money isn't everything. I know that no one lives forever, and there are some things I may not be able to do when I'm older. So, I now make time and budget for travel, one-time opportunities, and family. Time is the true treasure.

My vision for retirement is unrestricted time and spending freedom, not being on a fixed income. My version of spending freedom does not include working a W-2 but rather having my businesses produce income that replaces and surpasses the income I am currently earning while working for my employer. My umbrella business accommodates all my wealth-generating talents. I am a writer, speaker, and strategic planner specializing in leisure and luxurious rest. I have witnessed and experienced enough to understand that hustle culture is responsible for everyone looking good but not feeling good.

The United States was built on rewarding hard work and punishing laziness, while the rest of the world takes multiple mid-day breaks, is less hurried, and recognizes the redemptive power of long holidays and leave. Citizens who have never traveled outside the U.S. sometimes have no clue that we are the oddballs. Interestingly, the founders of this country patterned this work ethic after their British example, where the wealthy did not work hard at all. Yet, they rewarded the lower classes for their hard work and punished or loathed those with lesser means who absconded from laborious tasks. We've been doing it wrong for all the wrong reasons, and I have built my business into services that help others slow down and take time to enjoy the only life we have.

Since there are no do-overs in this life, I remind people to take care of themselves first so they can be the best they can be for others. Self-care isn't selfish; it's the optimization of oneself that produces clarity, creativity, better communities, and a better world. When we are tempted to drop things we've planned for ourselves when a loved one or employer comes running for our help with their hair on fire, we must remember the airplane safety advice: Put on your mask first before attempting to help others. It is for the good of all parties involved.

I offer a community to Black women who want to figure out

Dream Aloud!

what's next for them. We focus on planning streams of income that they can create to have freedom now and into retirement. The community includes one-on-one and group coaching with me, retreats to focus on ourselves and our budding businesses, and a networking sisterhood that cannot be duplicated.

Using my planning and strategy expertise, I offer retreat and reunion planning with logistics strategies and services to anyone who wishes to host a retreat to increase their business's revenue without having to do more work. My planning business is also a training ground for people who want to gain project management and event planning experience that could lead to an additional income stream. Helping others and myself equals purpose and passion at work.

My formula also includes a passive-income dream lifestyle. The passive income I receive from rental properties, investments, and partnerships (only those that support my desire to travel and my goals for time and spending freedom) allows me to continually increase my income, no matter where I am in the world. The bottom line is that now since I have aligned my purpose and passion, I have more freedom than ever before. Most of all, I'm happier because of the peace that has come with it.

If you're wondering how to discover what you were born to do, I recommend pulling back from all that distracts you and focusing on your goal to uncover the real you that you were created to be. Pulling back and focusing are vital to accomplishing any goal and ushering us into clarity and greater creativity in designing the life we want.

Many people quit their jobs during the pandemic and started their own businesses. Honestly, in 2020-2021, and even into portions of 2022, it was easy to hang a shingle outside your door or your proverbial virtual door and be in business, making lots of money. I started my business and wrote my book during this window of time. I always felt uneasy about advertising things I could do that needed to be quantifiable or qualifiable as a coach. I completed ICF training for coaching, and while that is a wonderful program that taught me the skills I need to walk alongside someone who wants to make changes in their lives, I found that the Black women I worked with were not interested in me simply asking them powerful questions and then leaving them to come up with their own solutions. They wanted a partner to help them take the dreams they had and turn them into realistic plans so they could become the best woman, businessperson, or CEO of their own lives that they could be. I have now adjusted my style to match their expectations and added Team Coaching and Mentoring credentials to my toolbox.

My clients are seasoned in the workforce. They live decent lives and are admired by many, but they feel something more awaits. Not only do they want to figure out what more is available, but they wonder if it's too late because they've spent fifteen, twenty, or even thirty years in the workforce. They have professional, high-profile jobs they can do with their eyes closed. They have pretty much seen it all as far as racism, sexism, and all the other "isms" and "schisms" that come along with working in Corporate America and other for-profit and nonprofit organizations, and many are looking forward to retirement within a decade or so. Those who have only a few years before retirement know they can stick it out because they've gotten over the hump. However, they are unable to determine what it would be like to have their own business or streams of income that would supplement their wages and replace them in retirement so they can have spending freedom.

My 20- and 30-something clients are like I was at their age.

Dream Aloud!

They are already thinking about the life they want when the kids are grown and have left home, when they no longer *have* to work, and what they can do to make their desires a reality. If this is you, I want you to know that I've learned what to do and what not to do without experiencing it all myself. Take the time to learn from someone else who went through your current situation before you. You'll never have the time, energy, or money to make all the mistakes yourself in order to live a good life filled with experience. Making all the mistakes yourself means you will have much more regret than any one person needs to bear.

When you take the time to learn from others who have been where you are and connect with others going through similar processes, you'll be more successful and find greater joy within a community. Don't stop there, though. Make sure you reach back and help someone who is going through—or will go through—what you've already conquered, which is why I write to you today.

When I was a young mother with a son, no child support, and a baby's daddy who wanted to punish me for not wanting to stay in an abusive relationship with him, I thought I was the only one who had been forced into motherhood. However, I learned through social media that I'm not the only one (I won't call myself a victim because we allow some things in our lives) who has fallen for the narcissistic okey-doke—when a man can't control his partner, he may impregnate her, thinking he can control her through his relationship with their child. The only time my son's father was interested in my and his son's whereabouts was when he thought he could keep me out of other relationships. His punishment for me was not to support me financially, and he rarely watched his child because he didn't want me to go out and have fun. Filled with a lot of resentment, I wasted too much time doing things to show him that we didn't need him. Although I'd left him, I still expected him to take care of his child. He didn't know his father and swore he would be the model father for his son. My parents came from single-parent homes, so I knew people make choices to follow the patterns of their parents or create their own paths. My focus was to shove his attempt to punish me in his face.

I dreamed of marrying someone else who would be an excellent father to my son. We would be a power couple, have many more kids and lots of money, and do all the things that would make my son's dad regret not being a father. I dreamed of the Shaquille O'Neal Effect, where his father tried to show up after he was drafted into the NBA, but Shaq rejected him and credited Phil, his stepdad, for being his father. I dreamed of revenge so sweet that I could not live my own life.

I was miserable back then. I complained to friends, and they complained back because we were all in the same spot. Older women with adult children, many of whom were grandparents, always responded curiously. When I complained about feeling wronged and mistreated, they always replied, "You'll make it," accompanied by a nonchalant look.

Why were they all saying the same thing in the same way? Many didn't even know each other. If I hadn't played my part in the situation, I wouldn't be burdened with all the responsibility. I would have felt better if they had told me I made my bed, so I had to lie in it. I was well aware that I should have walked away when I saw the first sign of narcissism when we started dating. Didn't they understand what was going on in my life? Didn't they know that this man was hurting my child every time he said he was coming to pick him up and never showed up?

Dream Aloud!

"You'll make it," was all I heard from seasoned folks. I thought about my grandmother, who had given birth to seven children, probably not under the best conditions. Six of them were with her second husband, who supported her inconsistently. She had three jobs: a coat factory job in town, doing hair at home for her clients, and sewing for others. She was an excellent cook who prepared meals for her family and others since childhood. Her role was cooking and caring for the children of those who worked on her mother's farm, as she was prone to fainting in the field from the intense South Carolina heat. She managed to raise her children, spend time with her friends and family, and be a happy (or at least content) person.

When I was growing up, even though they were separated and living in different cities, my grandfather would visit his children and grandchildren on holidays and weekends at Grandma's house. Little did I know, the house he came to for dinner with us was the one that HE still owned and paid yearly taxes on.

The lesson in the story: The women I'd talked to may have felt the way I did when they were young, but they were experiencing the joys of motherhood in their later years because they answered the call of long nights, short money, and self-sacrifice. I could have learned how to enjoy more of my son's childhood if I had asked them for their advice. If I had just stopped to think about those ladies who said, "You'll make it," I wouldn't have seen them as insensitive. I would have looked at them through a different lens. They were women who had been through what I had been through, and if I had just looked at their lives, their happiness, and their pride in their children, I would have known that I, too, could have that as a result of my sacrifice. The minute I decided to go that way, life got a lot easier.

Kendra Newman

On the day of my father's funeral, I sat in the family car with my friend Keywanda, waiting for my husband and uncles to join us before the caravan of cars began our journey to the cemetery. My cousin opened my door to tell me that someone wanted to speak with me. It was my baby's daddy. We didn't talk, but I was aware that he and his wife had contributed to the cost of the burial plot. He stood about ten yards away, patting his check, and I used sign language to respond, "Thank you." Then Cousin Omar closed the door.

That day, Keywanda and I had planned to go to *The Color Purple* musical for a girls' weekend, but those plans changed into a celebration of life for the great man who raised me.

"Girl, we don't need to see *The Color Purple*. There's Mister in that scene where Celie sees him across the field after finally doing the right thing by her," I told her while laughing and pointing toward my baby's daddy

While I no longer harbor hatred in my heart toward him, I still have no desire to hear the apology he has told my son he wants to extend to me. I do, however, forgive him and am glad he and our son are working out their issues. Now, when I witness the stress of young mothers wronged by selfish fathers, I think of the ladies who calmly assured me that I would make it—they will not only prevail but also be strengthened by their experiences.

STOCK UP ON MENTORS

What does that have to do with your lifestyle and livelihood? It's the same when you go through microaggressions at work, face ill-treatment, and are second-guessed for being the only Black woman in your position within your organization. While you may be the only Black person working there, you're not the

Dream Aloud!

only one who has faced what you're dealing with. Take advice from those who have successfully made it through the process. Find a mentor who can help prepare you to handle everything that will come your way in your career or business.

Mentors come in different flavors, stations, and containers. They do not have to be another Black woman, but it helps to have someone who understands the barriers set for Black women and is familiar with our plight. This is not the time to have to explain what you are experiencing and feeling. You need someone who knows these things well so you can focus on solutions. The problem you're facing is most likely new to you, but a mentor has seen it all before and can give you advice on how to resolve an issue that would take you months or years to figure out on your own. Collapse your problem-solving time with a mentor.

I was tired of not having my voice heard in meetings. So, I called up a senior HR advisor, not to speak to her as an HR person or an employee, but as a Black woman. I told her that my boss and his boss would cut me off each time I spoke during our weekly check-ins and how I felt defeated whenever I left those meetings. She immediately told me that I had given up my power. When I was cut off, I wouldn't say, "Excuse me, I was speaking," or speak over them instead of stopping when they interrupted me. She reminded me that I had a right to do that. She told me about a time a co-worker would rephrase everything she said in their meetings. Eventually, she stopped him, saying, "Excuse me, I can speak for myself." The minute I took her advice, choosing to speak louder and not allow them to cut me off while I was speaking, I felt better. However, after the first meeting of me doing this, I went back to my desk thinking, *I wonder when Jim is going to come in here and tell me how rude*

47

Kendra Newman

I was. To my surprise, when he reached my door, he said, "Great meeting today. That's the person I've been looking for!" Who knew being assertive was respected in my office? Certainly not me until that day. I'd already been in the workforce for twelve years. Just imagine if I'd had a mentor before this.

The problem is I didn't think I needed a mentor before then. Until I became a director with a title, I was judged primarily by my ability to manage and teach technology. I had done well for twelve years and two additional years at another company before I landed in higher education, not knowing that being recognized for doing well was a compliment. Even better is having someone who speaks highly of you in rooms you are not in. That is called sponsorship.

Sponsors and mentors are two totally different things. A sponsor is someone who has faith in what you do. This person has seen your value and is willing to tell others they value you. It quickly became apparent that until I moved from one university division to another to become a director, I had sponsors who would speak my name and recommend me for things. Granted, some sponsors were better than others, but even the least effective sponsors proved better than having no sponsor. In hindsight, I now know that a mentor would have helped me grasp the importance of sponsorship and identify my sponsors. The lack of sponsorship is a major, if not the number one, reason to act on your exit strategy. Without sponsors, it will be impossible for you to thrive in an organization. Survival should be something other than the goal of your career.

TIP: We may never really understand the power of sponsorship until we find ourselves without it. That's when it became all too clear to me. Let me save you some pain and possibly pay. Stay connected with people who want to mentor

Dream Aloud!

you and have good things to say about you. Unfortunately, most work environments don't provide a level playing field. If you do not have allies in your office or at a higher level, it's time to find a new place of employment.

Do you have sponsorship in your current organization? If you answered yes, list them and the ways they sponsor. See the example below.

Sponsor: K. Newman	Sponsorship: Recommends me for projects and assigns me to high-profile undertakings

Do you have mentors? If you answered yes, list them and the type of mentorship provided. See the following example.

Sponsor: K. Newman	Mentorship: Informal advice from a Black woman professional in higher education.

Kendra Newman

Sponsorship is usually out of your hands, as it is a decision made by those in places and spaces you are not. Think Joe Biden and Kamala Harris. Joe Biden—pushed out of the running for a second term by his own party—could have finished his presidency looking out for only himself. Instead, we see him rooting for Harris, including her name in accomplishments he can claim as his own, and letting the world know she is a competent and worthy presidential candidate. He puts in good words with his friends, constituents, and colleagues for her. Like Kamala, I've found older white men—with nothing to prove and not in competition with me—to be the best sponsors in my career. Perhaps this is true because older white men are at the top of the higher education tower and generally have headed the departments and organizations where I've worked. These are the people who have seen my work and confidently recommend or vouch for me when I've needed in-house endorsements, recommendations, or references while looking for new employment.

Mentorship is an area in which you can take charge of yourself. Just asking for and receiving advice informally is a type of mentorship. If you do nothing else, ask for help from trustworthy people. Consider seeking advice from professionals in your field, those who have been in your organization and possess greater insight than you, other men and women with a culture similar to yours, and someone of the same gender. You or your job can formally initiate mentorship with someone willing to meet with you consistently, either for free or a fee. Goals are set with objectives to be completed over time. This is a commitment for both the mentor and the mentee. Be sure you are ready and willing to fulfill the requirements before agreeing to engage. At the very least, be an adult. If you are unable to continue adhering to your agreement, don't waste anyone's time.

Dream Aloud!

Build your mentorship roster. Write three descriptions of the mentors you would like to have to improve your career or business.

Mentorship Description:

If you are ready to live the life of your dreams, the way you make a living must be suitable for such a life. Start by making a commitment to yourself. Promise yourself to live life to the fullest, including having a livelihood that aligns with your desired lifestyle. No more stuffing little pieces of life into the cracks and open spaces that a job schedule allows.

Decide to create a livelihood with work and income streams that will allow you the time and spending freedom to live on your terms, both now and into retirement. Know that it won't be easy—nothing worth having is—but your plan to get there can be easy. Complicated calculations and plans are not necessary to reach your goal. The formula is simple; some may think it's way too easy, and it is. Just remember, life throws us challenges and curveballs that we may not have anticipated. That's where the strategy to stay on course comes in. I've made the process easy so that it does not become a distraction when life happens. Obstacles are inevitable; don't let them stop you. Make your memory of each encounter a lesson learned so you can refer to them when other obstacles arise. Even use your experiences to mentor others because, of course, you shouldn't just be mentored. Return the favor and mentor someone else.

When I started my business, I chose to keep my 9-to-5 for several reasons. I like what I do, and my job provides health insurance for me and my husband, who owns his own business. People quit their jobs in 2020 (the same year I started my business) to start or continue their entrepreneurial journey full-time. Others had been let go from their employment and decided to do their own thing. Since then, I've encountered many who have either returned to the workforce or are hustling to pay their bills. Perhaps they were hustling to pay their bills before 2020. Whatever the case, that will not be me. My commitment to myself and my clients is to always operate with integrity because I belong to the Most High. It's important to me to treat others with respect and live a life that pleases God, my only true audience. If I please God, I will have lived the life I wanted to live while letting my gifts create income and impact for myself and others.

There have been coaches and people who have said that a person is doing too much and needs to pick one thing. I was told you have to have an outcome for your product or service that people want. I agree with this advice, but not every formula is for everyone. How can I contain my multiple talents into one thing? There's a way to dispense my various talents and work them MY way. We must find it for ourselves.

For me, I was born a cheerleader to encourage other people to be all they were created to be. I can see your gifts and talents before you do. My gift is to recognize what you can do with what is in your toolbox of experiences, gifts, and talents to live a life of freedom in line with your dreams. I'm also a gifted

Dream Aloud!

writer, speaker, storyteller, and most of all, I AM HELP. I'm a logistics person who can see all angles, create a flexible plan to adjust to any circumstance, and make what you want a reality. That's why I'm relied upon for reunions and retreats by busy hosts who want to show up and enjoy themselves. I am like that wedding planner without the bridezillas or momzillas. My company helps hosts show up the same way grooms show up for weddings—having all the fun minus the stress.

Please note it hasn't been all roses, and life requires adjustments at various stages. Consider this book your mentorship from me, written to help you avoid some of the pitfalls (many of which are detailed here in my stories) and hopefully not wait until midlife to make the changes you need to live fully, out loud, and in color. For those of you who are at the midlife point and are just starting to make the life and livelihood shifts to live the life of your dreams, do not be discouraged. I, too, spent a long time holding onto my "good job" and neglecting my heart's longing. It's not too late! NOW is the time to start living for you and manifest your magnificence for monetary gain.

Are you ready to get started on this journey? I'll take you on a stroll down my memory lane of employment and lifestyle to let you know you are not alone. May my candid accounts steer you into taking action to redesign your life to match your dreams—the dreams placed in your heart to help you answer the call on your life, which is to live on purpose with passion. Then, your living will be impactful and not in vain. The moment you move towards fulfilling your purpose, the universe will begin to work with you to deliver the people and things you need to successfully become the person you were meant to be. Decide in your heart to move forward and start taking action. Then, watch as people and opportunities show up.

What Do You Believe?

As a little girl, I knew I was supposed to be successful. So much so that I would lie in my bed and pray, "Lord, don't let me become so rich that I forget about You." At eight or nine years old, I prayed like that, and to this day, I'm not sure why I prayed that prayer, but I am convinced it came from some teaching that was imparted indirectly—most likely from my church. Have you ever said, "The Lord helps those who help themselves"? What about "Cleanliness is next to godliness"? These are not quotes from any holy scripture or religion but a "belief" or agreement with the status quo.

I had long believed that many members of the technology sector could work from home. I even made a post about this in 2011. I dreamed of what it would be like not to have to commute fifty miles to work every day for a worthwhile salary and how much more I could get done at home. For instance, I wanted more time to take care of my garden. I talked to entrepreneurs and some W-2 workers—or "telecommuters" as we called them back then—to get an idea if my inkling was correct. I wanted to say goodbye to commuting in highway traffic or on crowded public transportation when the weather was bad. Not only that, but I was tired of spending extra money on gas and tolls. Then, I had to worry about sitting next to ill co-workers without enough sick time to stay home. When I considered all these things, working from home seemed ideal.

Most businesses did not offer telecommuting as an option to their employees. They wanted people in the office so they knew the employees were doing the work they were getting paid to do. The truth is, in technology, the work has to get done, or EVERYTHING will come to a halt. When I first started in this business as a software engineer at Philadelphia Airport, whenever the network went down, the accountants, airport operations staff, and personnel departments worked on tasks that did not require using their computers. Today, everything requires online access, and technology staff members who do not pull their weight get noticed in record time.

"We have the technology to work from home," I would say with each passing year. Many of our meetings were via teleconferencing at our office desks, as not everyone worked in the same building. The help desk staff took over computers remotely to repair the desktop issues of clients in other cities and countries. Then, March 2020 hit us like a ton of bricks. We were under shelter-in-place orders. In two weeks, the world quickly pivoted from "Working from home will not work" to adapting to doing just that. The first weeks were filled with figuring it out as we went about doing our jobs, rearranging meetings from in-person to online, getting the right software applications in place, and determining what was working and what needed to change

Dream Aloud!

for the better. Technology has made all of this rapid change possible. Those who were familiar with online conferencing and collaborative software fared well.

I had finally been able to prove my telecommuting in tech theory, and the entire world helped. Many never thought it would work, but when forced, they got in line and became believers.

"It always seems impossible until it's done."
~ Nelson Mandela

What are some things you thought were impossible but aren't? What do you still think is impossible?

_____
_____
_____
_____
_____
_____
_____
_____
_____
_____
_____
_____

Kendra Newman

Let's analyze why you thought those things were impossible and what changed your mind.

I was in my 11th-grade history class, and the topic was current affairs. Somehow, the Cosby Show came up, and I told the teacher, "That's not true in real life." My comment was about people my age having two professional parents: a doctor and a lawyer. If I were to analyze my statement even deeper, I probably was referring to African American couples with children, as my experience was working class. We had a few doctors, lawyers, and other professionals in our circle, but none that I knew were married to one another. My 16-year-old experience shaped my belief that having just one prestigious professional per family was plenty and probably rare. The instant the words rolled off my tongue, my teacher asked, "Why not?" and I didn't have an answer. Immediately, I confronted my thinking and knew right away that the only thing that made me say two professional households did not exist—except in TV fantasy land—was because I'd never seen it before, not even on television except for the uber-rich couple Alan and Monica Quartermaine, who were medical doctors on the soap opera *General Hospital*.

My two-professional household theory was never taught but became a solid belief due to my surroundings. That day's lesson taught me how easily belief systems are formed and can remain throughout a lifetime if we aren't exposed to other points of view or challenged to think differently. What do you still think is impossible? I ask myself this question regularly. Then I sit with my thought of "impossible" and ask myself, *Is that really true?* Now it's your turn. What did you list as impossible for you earlier in this chapter? Is it truly impossible, or do you need to look at things in a different way? Will you need to change your approach to making what seems impossible possible?

Dream Aloud!

May I suggest you analyze what you believe—not what you SAY you believe, but what you genuinely believe in your heart. This is no time to be politically correct or sugarcoat things.

Like me, you may have formed some beliefs simply by observing. What beliefs did you derive from your childhood home, community, school, job, and nation?

_____
_____
_____
_____
_____
_____
_____
_____
_____
_____
_____
_____
_____
_____
_____

Kendra Newman

Are your beliefs true not just for you but for mankind, too? If not, what do others believe, and why?

_____
_____
_____
_____
_____
_____
_____
_____
_____
_____
_____
_____
_____
_____
_____

These questions aren't asked in expectation of you solving the world's problems but rather to help you get a good picture of how experience and exposure shape our belief systems. Once we are aware, we are more likely to change our outlook for the better by removing a system of beliefs that holds us back from living better.

Dream Aloud!

FALSE BELIEFS

Did you know there are only two types of genuine fear? That's right; we are born only with the fear of falling and loud noises (and I question the first one). If you think about all the fears you may have or google a list of phobias rooted in fear, you may wonder how there could be only two natural fears. Why does it feel like there are zillions, and when did we start believing the lies of others? The "others" probably developed their fears from their own experiences and opinions of others. These fears are then placed on us throughout our lives through observation and influence. Add all of this to our experiences, and we have a stew of fears that hold us back from our wildest dreams and even some of the simplest tasks.

Getting to the root of the catalyst for our fears can answer the question we must ask each time fear threatens to stop us: Should I steer clear of a person or situation, or is this a false fear hindering my progress?

Neither of my parents knew how to swim. They feared drowning because both had witnessed people they knew going under and not resurfacing. On the day my dad was determined to learn to swim as a teen, someone drowned at the sand wash––a place with undercurrents and steep drop-offs. He said that was enough for him not to get in the water to learn that day or ever. His experience instilled a fear of drowning and ultimately dying while swimming. My mother, on the other hand, was a mother. Her fear may have begun as a fear of drowning, but as a mother, the fear is that your child could drown because they cannot swim. Even worse, she and her husband would not be able to save their child because they did not know how to swim themselves.

Kendra Newman

My parents allowed me to go on swimming trips to the lake and the ocean at summer camp. Mom schooled me on not going out into the water past my chest at the lake or my waist in the ocean. She warned that the waves could knock me down and pull anyone out to sea with their undertow. Not wanting to pass on her fear of bodies of water to me, she took me to swim class, where I learned to float, doggie paddle, and do the simple breaststroke.

What does this have to do with building the livelihood you want? EVERYTHING. Fear stops us from doing what we want. What fear do you have concerning making changes in your career or business that caused you to purchase this book? Chances are you want to figure out how to start creating new income streams for yourself without losing everything. You may want to know if you should stay in your current position or try your hand at another company. Or perhaps you're worried about taking a bigger risk and wondering if it will be worth it. What if it doesn't work? Could you lose money, seniority, or your shirt? Now, ask yourself why you think any of this will happen. Maybe you've tried before, and something similar happened to you. Perhaps you've witnessed the experiences of other people who went after their dreams and ended up on Skid Row. Our fears, as well as our optimism, are based on beliefs we have. My examples of swimming and hanging around bodies of water reflect both the fears and optimism of my parents and, most likely, their parents.

As an 8th-generation Black person living in the United States, my fear of swimming is most likely rooted in slavery. Not only were the enslaved not permitted to learn to read for fear that they would acquire information that could help them gain their freedom, but they were also not allowed to learn to swim.

Dream Aloud!

I mean, what better way to escape the plantation or breeding farm than to swim out to where bloodhounds could not pick up your scent as you crossed the Ohio River? Then, the saying, "Black people don't swim," was passed down, suggesting to each generation that swimming is not for Black folks. However, in reality, swimming was snatched from them.

Swimming is like riding a bike. Watching someone else do it does not make the watcher able to swim. It's just the same as watching someone else ride a bike. Until you do it yourself, you're just a spectator. Watching the master's family enjoy the lake doesn't help much. One may learn a bit from someone who explains what to do once the waters have been entered, but that is not enough. Most coastal Africans could swim and, therefore, taught their children. Verbal history tells of my fifth great-grandfather being thrown overboard from the human cargo ship on which he arrived for sport. He swam ashore, was recaptured approximately three miles from Charleston, South Carolina, and sold to the Newman plantation in Chesterfield County.

Now imagine my great, great, great, great, great-grandfather arriving on the land of his owner. It was not near the ocean and was miles from the Pee Dee River that ran through the county, but even if there were a lake on the estate, the enslaved would not be permitted to wade in the water. The skill of swimming most likely died with him, as he would have been penalized for swimming, not to mention for teaching his children and others. The knowledge of swimming may have died with him and remained a mystery for six generations until my parents invested in swim lessons for me.

My son, on the other hand, attended schools with pools. He began taking swim classes as part of the physical education program at his elementary school and continued in high school.

He's never had a fear of water, and he ignored my lake and ocean warnings that stemmed from his grandparents' fear. He's had the opportunity to learn to swim and learn about water safety from a different approach.

Do you see how the experience of preserving one's life (not being killed for swimming) led to a mantra of "Black people don't swim"? Generations of people who were unable to traverse bodies of water yielded fears of drowning and, most of all, death. This is just one example of how beliefs are established and become our truths or self-fulfilling prophecies.

Perhaps you can relate to this example. What are your stories that show the 'why' behind some things you believe? It's important to examine as many as possible to free yourself from false beliefs. I know you're looking to tackle big world problems, but trust me, when we identify, test, and address our genuine fears and their origins, we set a foundation to support the lifestyle-driven livelihood we want to create.

Setting a foundation to build the lifestyle, legacy, and livelihood of your dreams is paramount for creating lasting change that will positively impact your life and the lives of those you love. Do not skip the root work; it will set you up for repeated success. Now, here is your heart work:

Make a list of the fears you have and ask yourself why you have these fears. Ask the following questions:

- What is the real fear I have around this issue? (Remember, my parents' issue was not a fear of swimming. It was a fear of drowning, and at the root, it was the fear of dying.)

Dream Aloud!

- Once you get to the root fear, list your "What Ifs." ("What if my child gets into trouble in the water, and I cannot get to her?" That was my mother's.)
- Now, ask yourself the likelihood of each "What If" and how you can mitigate or minimize the impact of your fear becoming a reality. (My parents mitigated this by enrolling me in swim class.)

How Do You See Yourself?

There is a biblical story about the Israelites who left Egypt and wandered in the wilderness for forty years because they would not follow God's promptings to make a forty-day trip. After forty years of benefiting from the miraculous—in a wilderness, no less—you would think the people would be willing to go into the land given to them. The land promised to them was fertile for planting, raising cattle, and accessing natural spices.

Instead of focusing on the benefits of the land and having confidence that they owned it, they counted all that was against them. The fact that giants already lived in the land made them conjure up "What If" visions, such as "What if we go over there and have to fight these giants for the land?" "What if the giants kill us?!" "What if we can't grow grapes and melons like we see right now in the land?" Only two out of twelve land surveyors had the confidence and courage to believe and state that they could move into the land, defend themselves if necessary, and cultivate it to live off its produce.

Kendra Newman

The story is often told from the point of view of Joshua and Kaleb, the two who declared they could take over the land. Let's zero in on the other ten. They were on the survey squad for a reason. Let's say someone was probably a horticulturist, another a herdsman, a beekeeper, an engineer, an architect, etc. Each was assigned to do the work in which they specialized. They provided a great report on what the land offered, from living conditions to recreation. They put together their pros and cons list, but the pros substantially outweighed the cons. However, the very first item on the cons list was GIANTS. Now, pretend to be a fly on the wall. "I'm a farmer, not a fighter!" says the horticulturist. "Exactly! I'm an engineer and only know how to build things," says the other. Their responses are evidence of their thinking. They began to speak negatively to themselves and others until they became incapable, IN THEIR OWN EYES, of doing what God had already said they could do.

How do you see yourself? Are you qualified for that position that will provide the raise you desire, but you're afraid that being the only person of color in the room will cost you? Or have you turned down a position offered to you because you didn't want to be bothered with all the junk that came along with it? How about your own business? How many events have you planned, decorated, and run for yourself and your friends but still refuse to start your own event planning or design business because everyone else you know in the industry has a degree in that area? Do these things make you feel less than qualified? Do they cause you to shrink? If so, let's address the GIANT ON YOUR REAL ESTATE. What would any person who has a right to a property do if they found squatters?

The absence of fear is optional when completing the work assigned to you. You only need courage.

Dream Aloud!

There's a story of women in Numbers 27 of the Bible. Back then, only men were counted in the census for the Israelites. If a man died without having sons, his land would be given to his brothers because women were expected to marry and leave their tribe. Zelophehad was a girl dad, and when he died, his five daughters went to the men who were doling out land according to the male-only census and requested what was rightfully theirs. Their father had followed the rules while living, and they contended that they, being heirs of their father, had a right to the land bequeathed to him. The five sisters saw themselves as well qualified to inherit their father's land. Because they saw themselves as worthy of their birthright and were willing to speak up about it, they got what they desired and deserved. May you see yourself as worthy of what you were born to do, be, see, and have. Stand up for yourself and receive what is meant for you.

Set your own valuation of your possessions. When we allow others to determine our value and that of our possessions, it shows that our view of ourselves may be lower than necessary to live our best lives.

I'm from a rural town where I've returned to live in my mid-30s. My feelings about the location differ from most of my compadres simply because of how my father felt about it. My father moved to Mizpah in the 1940s. It had a majority Italian population that overtook the original Jewish settlement. Railroad tracks and Railroad Boulevard separated Black homes on the north side of town from the white homes south of the tracks. Gigantic City (an area smaller than Mizpah) made up the eastern border of the Black neighborhood; this, too, was an Italian neighborhood. A single artery, West Point, runs through Mizpah, and one needs to drive through the southern portion of Gigantic City to enter or leave.

Kendra Newman

Blacks were not permitted to live in the county seat, so they were relegated to Mizpah and its two neighboring towns: Richland to the west and Newtonville to the north. During an unprecedented forest fire, everyone in the neighborhood—now predominantly Black on both sides of the railroad tracks—understood the implications of having limited access and exits. Anyone who lived "down the bottom," the very tip of the north side that borders Newtonville, would have been trapped if the fire had started on the south side of West Point, as every street becomes a dead end at the forest edge instead of a passageway into the neighboring burrow to the north.

Not only were Black folks relegated to the north side, but they were placed in jeopardy before and after the great fire, as there still was no outlet "down the bottom." Growing up, the neighboring towns looked down on Mizpah. Black citizens of the neighboring towns turned up their noses, too, but many took every chance they could to spend time there. Many of my neighbors abandoned the homes their parents and grandparents worked hard to purchase and ran off to other towns and states with more to offer. In typical gentrification fashion, outside powers pounced on my little town after the community warriors aged and passed away. Children and grandchildren failed to pay taxes on their grandparents' homes and lost them to auction. Many ran them into the ground with no plan to maintain or even make a profit from the sale of modest structures that sat on acres of land. Those smart enough to sell took their money and ran, never looking back. They were happy to leave the place they were told was cursed, even though the word Mizpah means watchtower, which is a loose translation of the Hebrew saying, "May God watch over you." When we don't know the meaning of things, we tend to misplace value because we lack the ability

Dream Aloud!

to see the significance of holding on with a vision of improving one's circumstances.

Dirt roads have been paved, natural gas lines have been laid, and abandoned houses have been sold to the highest bidder for pennies on the dollar. The vision of one investor has made him a rich man by flipping houses for a great profit while keeping them affordable for buyers. The neighborhood looks good, and "The Bottom" is filled with new and renovated homes with manicured lawns and picket fences. The place looks pretty close to Mayberry, with an animal rescue farm. Horses and chickens are commonplace again. Only now have former citizens and members of neighboring communities begun to think that Mizpah may indeed be the metropolis of good, but only after new, mostly white residents began moving in and speaking positively about it.

I, too, had this embedded prejudice against my culture and had no idea that it existed. I was proud to have attended a good school and never felt it strange to be one of only four or fewer Black students in my class of twenty or more. Never once did it occur to me that there were little to no Latinx or Asian children in our school. The only teachers who looked like me were the Home Economics teacher and substitutes, and I never found that strange. That school, of course, was in the township seat that hadn't allowed Blacks to live there just over a few decades prior to my birth, and it never occurred to me that only a handful of Black children lived in the town when I attended. The rest of us lived in the surrounding towns where our parents grew up, and we never questioned why our towns were mostly Black but our school was the total opposite. It never occurred to me that all of the resources were being hoarded in the township seat while the rest of us were able to use them when we made the fifteen-

Kendra Newman

minute drive to the county seat. I was a good student and a rule follower who found favor with most of my teachers. Rule followers do what is right. I was judged on the content of my character and didn't buck the system much, and when I did, I was excused because I was a "good kid" for the most part.

    I remember bragging about our good school system and everyone getting along. Sure, there were days when my mother, aunt, and I walked into restaurants in the county seat for lunch, and everyone stopped to stare. I'd always ask to leave, but Mom said we couldn't run every time someone thought we were out of our place. "We have a right to eat where we want," she would say. I thought those people were the exception. I wanted the same things my schoolmates wanted; I knew they had more of what we both wanted, and I didn't find anything wrong with that. My habitual thinking carried me through college and my career. I thought if I worked hard and followed the rules, I would be recognized just as I had been in school. Instead, I was overworked and received very little recognition. Eventually, I felt unseen and devalued despite knowing I knew more than many of my peers.

    My peers worked hard to grab a spot. They were applying for and getting promotions I didn't even know I should have been applying for. People I had trained were moving upward while I was stuck in the same place. It was taking a toll on my psyche. The more I was overlooked, the more I shrank, and the more I shrank, the more frustrated I became with people who were "failing up."

    The quote, "One person's trash is someone else's treasure," should be applied to every area of your life. In the case of my hometown, the people who lived there believed the lie that nothing good could come from Mizpah and left in search of better. Others saw the value of rural living—the absence of HOA fees and nosy neighbors—and had enough vision to build the homes in the neighborhood that they envisioned.

Without a vision, the people perish. My vision for getting ahead in the workplace is based on what worked for me in the classroom. Teachers are trained to recognize the potential in someone and bring it out, and it helps if they like their students. In the workplace, it is the employees' job to make sure their work is recognized. You must toot your own horn and speak up. Lean in, as Sheryl Sandberg says. If I don't value what's inside of me, no one else will. Supervisors are too busy working on their own upward mobility, and rightly so. Advocate for yourself. Most career opportunities come from relationships. It's not always the most qualified who get the promotion but the ones who are most congenial.

Don't take what goes on around you personally. Observe what is happening. Make the most honest evaluation of your situation that you can. Document all your accomplishments, go into your boss's office, and ask for what you deserve and want. Back up your request with facts and achievements. Don't get mad if they show you that they don't think you're worth it. Instead, get what you can get out of them while you work on your exit strategy. The organization you work for now may not value your experience and talent, but believe me, someone else will. You just need to know how best to provide your services and get paid royally.

UNCONDITIONING

Now that you've identified your beliefs and separated the good from the bad, it is time to undo some things. I've created an unconditioning approach that helps us dig deep into what we believe, do, or have, making it all make sense by stripping away our false beliefs. You are then ready to create the world you want with truths. Think of all the things you've heard your parents, teachers, and friends say that start with or contain the word "they," such as: "They don't want you to get ahead," "Seven secrets THEY don't want you to know about," and "They say you can't fight city hall." Who is "they"?

We hear some of these things for so long that we remove "they" altogether and start believing them as law. Do any of these sound familiar?

- You can't fight city hall.
- You don't question God.
- It's not what you know but who you know.

These statements may be true in many circumstances but not in every situation.

Worse than that, falling prey to what "they" say is the subconscious conditioning that happens daily without a word. As a Black woman living in the United States, I have been subjected to many subliminal messages from everyone I've encountered throughout my life. Please read my Sheryl Sandberg-like message: *"I HAVE WRITTEN THIS BOOK FROM THE LENS THROUGH WHICH I HAVE LIVED MY ENTIRE LIFE AS A BLACK WOMAN. This is not to negate or invalidate anyone else's experience. So, if you have not figured it out by now, my examples are those from my experience. This is not to say that there are no other points of view, but I can only write about my own."*

Dream Aloud!

You aren't the only one who needs unconditioning. Everyone has been conditioned in some way, shape, or form by their environment—at home, in their country, their community, and any other social hierarchy.

I had just accepted my dream job, and when I entered the office and began introducing myself to all the employees, there were whispers that I should not trust my boss and that he was a racist. Until that point, I had been judged by my work as a thorough and competent technology specialist, and I was hired to lead a team that would change the trajectory of the college with new technology—or so I thought. It began with being called everything except my director's title by faculty, deans, and other leadership. I had to correct introductions that included them referring to me as Kendra, the Tech Person, Substitute Tech Person with IT support, and even Tech Queen—anything to avoid recognizing my title and capabilities.

It turns out my supervisor was indeed a racist without a good clue of how to pretend he was not. He would address my Black male employee as "ma man" and make jokes that included comments about his friend's black cat named Mr. Clarence. The only Black member of Bruce Springsteen's band had the same name, minus the Mister. One day, during a one-on-one meeting in my supervisor's office, I began singing along with a rock song playing in the background. As I sang the words, my supervisor turned to his computer and, with his back to me, told me that he had something I would like better and then switched to a hip-hop station. When he turned back to face me, he gave a proud look of satisfaction from across his desk and proceeded to tell me that his kids liked Black music and hip-hop rap stuff. I made it my business to correct him, stating, "It's all Black music, including that rock song."

Kendra Newman

Where did he learn that? Did he think Black people only liked what he called Black music? Why did he think it was okay to say that to a Black person? It even got so bad that after he fired all the African American secretaries and administrative assistants in every department within the college, he rewrote their job listings with requirements for college degrees because he knew they didn't have any. After the layoffs, those same women and the people who were their friends said he was a racist, and his reputation began to precede him. His conditioning about who and what Black people were and their station in life was so deep that he called me into his office to tell me that he was tired of hearing racist comments about himself and wanted them to stop. He then informed me that he had called in the only other Black woman on his leadership team to tell her the same. When I asked him if he had only called the two of us—the Black people—into his office, his conditioning let him respond matter-of-factly and confidently, "Yes."

He had no idea that his discriminating actions were prejudiced, at the very least, if not verifying the allegations against him. It wasn't my job to teach him the error of his ways, but it was my job to understand that he had done many things to show he had class and race issues that skewed his point of view. It was evident to me from some things he had said and done over the years that he had a complex from growing up working-class in a section of the city that only held what they thought was superiority over the non-white people whom his parents and neighbors kept out of their neighborhood. It was more than obvious that he had spent a great deal of time measuring himself and his accomplishments against his colleagues in various departments. His frequent use of the word "pedigree," bragging about knowing someone in higher ranks, and inappropriate

Dream Aloud!

vernacular toward others shed light on his inferiority complex.

My pettiness made me play with his conditioned mind. I knew he was probably the first one in his family to earn a degree. I also knew he was likely a third-generation American. Yet, he had been conditioned to believe that all Black people were like the Black people that they kept out of their neighborhood. I took my opportunity that day to poke holes in his conditioning. I started by asking, "Isn't it interesting that you only asked the two Black people in your direct report portfolio?" I then let him know that I hadn't called him a racist, but his act of only calling us into his office could be perceived as racist. I proceeded with, "I can see why a racist rumor about you could have started, given that you've laid off every Black administrative assistant in each department except for the three you've demoted to front desk support in your major buildings."

Interesting fact: these women had been in their positions for decades and could run their departments with their eyes closed. Yet, they were laid off, and their job descriptions were written in such a way that they did not qualify to reapply because they lacked degrees. That's probably where the racist rumor started.

Perhaps those left employed saw that he had given himself a raise along with his new title immediately after ridding the college of these ladies and posting their positions for much less than the salary they had earned after years of tenure and promotion.

"These ladies had the opportunity to get degrees as university employees, but their concern was their children," I told him. "Who knew that a job they had done for most of their adult lives would require a degree with no experience and push them out of the university? Their children were probably the first ones in their families to have degrees, and that's most likely why they worked here for so long—for their children's future. So, they work for people who are the first in their families to earn a degree."

I was talking about him, and he knew it. When I made my last statement, he raised his hand as if to say, *Yes, I'm the first one in my family to get a degree.* I knew he had a bachelor's and a master's degree. I went on to tell him that not all Black people are the same. Not all Black people are uneducated and need to be schooled on what he had just learned while climbing the social and corporate ladder.

I took the liberty of telling him a bit about my lineage—that I come from a long line of PhDs, clergy, nurses, teachers, and a few in government leadership. Then I told him about the holders of JD credentials and my relationships—by blood and/or bond––to sitting judges up and down the East Coast, as well as my strong family legacy in South Carolina, with over ten generations living and working on American soil, many of whom served in leadership roles. When I saw him turn red, I knew I had made it even worse for myself because I was sure that the minute I left his office, he would go straight to Google to fact-check all that I'd told him. But it was true, and he demonstrated on many occasions that he despised those who had more status, pay, or experience than he did but thought they should not.

I left the office that day only after letting him know I didn't have a Doctor of Something degree simply because I wasn't interested in getting one. I also told him to tread lightly when accusing people of accusing him, as it might not look so good for him.

I tell you that story not to bring up racism in a sense but to show you that everyone has some conditioning. In most cases,

Dream Aloud!

it is not your assignment to reprogram anyone but yourself. This incident—and many more incidents with my supervisor—led me to get a certificate in diversity and inclusion, which was free at the university. I did it mostly to satisfy my curiosity about what makes people tick and why so many "privileged folks," who weren't much privileged outside of their skin color, feel the way they do. Curiosity made me enroll in the program, and the learning strategies I gained on how I could work around this issue to make my life easier as an employee are why I continue my work in Diversity, Equity, and Inclusion (DEI) spaces. I dedicated my spare time during weekends to get my certificate and work with people who wanted to make a difference and change systems. Not only did I learn a great deal about others, but I learned plenty about myself.

Clearly, I could see racism as a woman and a Black person. I could see why it hurt, and things needed to change for the better. Even though many felt we were in a post-racial society, what I was not aware of was my own privilege regarding ability. This course showed me how someone like my supervisor—a white man who did not come from privilege—could feel as if he had worked for everything and that people like me, who call him racist for no reason, just need to work on themselves. I began to look at my privilege concerning ability. I never stop at a step and ask myself how I am going to get into this building; I simply walk up the step. I never stop at a door and wait for someone to open it. I have the arms to do it for myself. This example opened my eyes to how people can ignore the suffering of others. If it is not an obstacle, then it goes unnoticed by the one who faces no challenge. Because I am not mentally, visually, or hearing impaired in ways that prevent me from taking advantage of certain opportunities, I am privileged in instances where others are not. Seeing myself as someone who doesn't worry about stairs, ramps, elevators, braille, or captions, I could see how someone with white skin could overlook the fact that everyone in the boardroom looks like him, especially when most boardrooms have a similar composition. It doesn't make it right, but it exposed truths that changed my approach to how I deal with people in the workplace and how I judge whether a workplace culture is conducive to the life that I want to live.

Some of us spend our time breaking down walls and systems because it is our calling. When it is not your calling to be a systemic catalyst for change, you need to evaluate the system and decide how you will fare there. Afterward, decide whether you will stay or go to a place where you are valued.

DON'T GET STUCK IN CONDITIONING

We've always done it that way. That's just the way it is. Those are some of the most dangerous words to hear or speak. Those who use these phrases most likely don't have a healthy view of change. Whether they fear, loathe, or avoid constant change matters not. The key is that when you hear these words, they indicate that change is not welcomed. If you're among the majority who think something is right because everyone else feels that same way, that is your indication to think it over and ask yourself what you believe to be true and why. Now, continue to integrate your thoughts on the matter. When and where did you learn to think this way? When change is not embraced, battles ensue. There will be an internal battle between your future self, who wants to step out of the box, and who you are right now. Your present persona has not seen anything new.

After acknowledging that our thinking may be off and

Dream Aloud!

validated by groupthink, it's important to change our thoughts and create new worlds of reality.

I once heard someone say, *Nothing happens in the Kingdom unless something is said.* What are you building for yourself with your words? Say what you want to see. And each time a thought that does not align with the kingdom you want to live in arises, stop that thought with words. Say out loud to yourself, *No, I will have this type of life.* Replace every negative thought with a positive one. This takes practice but works. Give yourself grace as you work through this. Write it, say it, visualize it. If you can see it, you can have it. This is why I suggest you WRITE what you want for your life, SPEAK what you've written out loud, and THINK or visualize what you've written and speak daily. The more you do it, the more real it becomes to you. This will change your mind's vision and get you in a position to believe you are truly worthy of what you want—because you are.

This will combat the waves of doubt that come from your past and the conditioned people, systems, and institutions that govern so much of our environment. It's your responsibility to combat this with what you know to be the truth of the life you desire and deserve.

Get a mantra or two. They are not just feel-good words; they have power. Saying them is good, but living by them is better. Decide now to speak your way into the life you want.

When my son was little, we prayed daily on our way to his school. The mantra/confession was: There is nothing that can happen to me today that God cannot handle. This mindset allowed us to do our work (in school and on the job) without worrying about the things that could distract us because God already had it under control. Even things that surprised us were not a surprise to the Most High, and therefore, we won.

Applying this kind of mantra requires plenty of unconditioning. If one has been raised to worry about every little thing, this mantra will take time, but it still works. You must be willing to put in the time to say some things that you want to be true for you but are not necessarily so at the time you begin to say them. The only thing I can say about this is to trust the process. It will feel odd and awkward at first, but keep saying it until you see it.

LIFE'S HIDDEN LESSONS

Lesson 1:
We all need unconditioning. Just remember, you cannot change anyone but yourself. Get what you need and move on quickly.

I hadn't really run into opposition until I got my first leadership position. Prior to that, I was more of a worker, and as long as I was smart and able to produce in the technology field, I was rewarded—or at least left alone. I had no idea of the importance of sponsorship until I had none.

Sponsors are people who speak your name positively to others in rooms where you are not. Apparently, I had sponsors for the first twelve years of my career, but I wasn't aware of it until I no longer had sponsorship. Trust me, while one may not understand the importance of sponsorship when they have it, it becomes quite apparent when it is missing.

My boss's conditioning for racism, as well as his propensity for pre-judging, was not just my problem. It was the problem of

Dream Aloud!

the whole department. He had managed to fool people for a while, but his past followed him, and we found out he was actually that type of person everywhere. After I put him in his place by talking about my class and status as a family, I became his personal target.

After more than ten years in my profession, receiving awards and recognition, I was treated as if I did not cut the mustard, and I began to believe what was being said. I questioned my competency, wondering how I had gotten so far off the mark.

A group for women of color met quarterly at the university, and I began to learn that what I was experiencing was not uncommon when a certain senior vice president spoke to us on a day when I absolutely needed to hear what she had to say. Her co-workers began to systematically use microaggressions against her to the point where she had to go back and remember who she was and the skills that she possessed. I almost broke down crying in that room because I knew then that it wasn't just me. It was a tactic being used against many women who looked like me. Why did it take me so long to realize that?

I had shed so many tears over my eight years as director, but I would not let them see me sweat. Working day and night to make sure I crossed every T and dotted every I was a heavier burden than necessary for someone who is skilled at her job. It's an unnecessary tax that many believe must be paid—the proverbial "Be twice as good." I was already twice as good as my colleagues and had the nerve to insult myself by falling for the okey-doke from a mediocre supervisor.

One day, while in my boss's office, he told me about all the dissatisfied faculty members who were working with me. When I let out a deep sigh, he asked me what I would like to say.

Kendra Newman

Knowing he was a liar and not really interested in what I had to say beyond holding it against me later, I replied, "Nothing." I got up from my seat and barely made it three doors down to my office. The minute I made it through the threshold, I closed the door behind me, locked it, sat in my chair, and let the tears flow.

I know I'm good at what I do, and I know I bring solutions to my departmental problems. I regularly go behind them and fix things because they decided they were capable of making better decisions. When they realize their ideas are lacking, to put it mildly, they put them in my lap to make things right. There are days when I've spent more than twelve hours in the office covering my behind and doing what they need, then doing my own job after hours.

There are eight departments spread across three campuses, and I have one employee (which later became two) because the dean's office claimed it did not have enough in the budget to fully staff a team to manage the integration of technology in the office, classroom, and research labs. The consistent routine of hiring more faculty and staff in other departments—for which I would be responsible for providing tech support—was evidence that I was overworked, underpaid, and perhaps set up to fail. But I refused to fail. I refused to fail because my reputation was on the line. I refused to fail because I was a single parent with a son in college, bills to pay, and a career that had been stellar until then.

I used my supervisor's "critique" of me against him for my benefit. My response to him telling me that he was looking for a Black mentor for me and could not find any was registering for the Black Enterprise Women of Power Summit. How could he argue with me attending a three-day event where there would be plenty of powerful Black women and coaching sessions? He agreed to send me, and I went.

While I was there, I heard similar stories of capable Black women being sabotaged, not treated well, and made to remain "in their place". Unfortunately, there were women of color who had doors opened for them. However, they pulled up the ladder after they'd climbed it and shut the door once they got in. The goal should be to pull more chairs up to the table so that more people of color and diversity can be in boardrooms.

One particular speaker seemed to speak directly to my situation as she discussed her time at a particular organization. She talked about losing everything at the end of her divorce and not being happy in her job, as she was treated poorly. Ever the introvert, I usually take notes and apply them to my life without speaking to the people who deliver the words. However, I felt I needed to speak to her, and once I approached the stage, I thanked her for her transparency and began to tell her what I was going through. My summary of being overworked, underpaid, and understaffed with the little equipment I needed was wearing me down. Yet, I kept making things work because I wouldn't let any responsibility fall. She stopped me mid-sentence and simply said, "Move on. Your work is done there."

Imagine my shock. My responsibilities, funded by my job, ran through my head. I thought to myself, *How will I be able to support myself? How can I move on? They have great benefits at my job, and I've been there for so long. How can I do that?* Over the next year, those questions continued to echo in my mind.

To top it off, when I returned, I was beginning a leadership course at the university. I'd asked to go the year before, and my supervisor, who did not know it existed, chose three other people to attend. Then, I was approved to go the second year. During one of my weekly one-on-one put-down sessions, I was told of all the people dissatisfied with my work. For my 360 evaluation, a component of the leadership course, I selected all the people my supervisor had identified as dissatisfied. Of course, as my supervisor, he also had to submit his review of my work.

Weeks later, I sat in the office of one of my ex-coworkers who had gone through the program and worked with the team to review the 360s with leadership mentees. As we looked over the results of the people my supervisor said didn't like me and were not satisfied with my work, the reviews stated otherwise. They gave me great reviews. His review, however, was less positive.

I sat in the chair across from Scott and cried. I felt hopeless because it was obvious that the person who wrote my review was also my antagonist. He had no intention of helping me improve, nor did he find anything wrong with what I was doing. He was punishing me for being what he called a pedigree higher than his. Now, I could have gone to HR, but it had become quite clear what happened to many in our department who filed complaints. HR was not our friend. HR staff were employed by the organization, and they were employees who wanted to keep their jobs, too. So, I decided to devise a plan to get everything I could out of the department before leaving.

Approximately a year later, executive leadership found out my supervisor wasn't as good as he had been pretending to be and that his financial records could have been better. All of a sudden, he left to work for the university's medical school. Isn't it interesting that after six months in medical school, he went out on medical leave and, upon his return, was gone? This man used people of color to fire other people of color. He was not a good supervisor to any of his staff except one. When he finally left, and we reported directly to the acting dean, it was clear to all his

Dream Aloud!

direct reports that we had been oppressed. We had no idea he ruled with such an iron fist until we experienced someone else who did not. The biggest lesson I learned is that you cannot change people's thoughts or beliefs. As the speaker at the Black Enterprise Women of Power Summit advised, I should have moved on because my work was done there. I've learned that I should move when prompted. I didn't have to suffer through eight years of unfair evaluations, little or no pay or raises, and less money to match my 401b and 401k because of one person's personality.

I've also learned that systemic organizational issues don't change with leadership. Life was still the same for me when he and the dean left. Wow.

One of the greatest lessons came while I worked as a director. Barack Obama was president, and I watched everything done to him—the credit they didn't give him for good things, the blame they placed on him for bad things, and even criticizing him for wearing, in their opinion, a bad suit. I learned how to respond by watching the Obamas. No, I'm not as good as them. It's about the saying, "When they go low, we go high." I reminded myself of that, but the only difference was when they went low, I stayed even.

Lesson 2:
We meet the same people in every organization we serve.

You'll run into the same people no matter where you work, worship, or recreate. They may have different names and faces, but they will rub you the same way.

When my department was finally rid of my insecure,

mediocre boss, who kept me in tears when no one was looking, he was replaced by an unqualified liar of a woman who was, for the record, not white. She had the same issues as my previous boss but played the game a little differently. Coworkers changed, but the backbiting and stabbing continued.

When I finally moved to another higher education organization, I chose to work for a department led by someone tired of playing the game. I accepted a position that has taken me out of the line of fire. The politics at this institution are the same as those at my former one, but I've taken a position and title that don't require tapping as hard or as long. I can see the games being played, but I am only a spectator.

My concern is always my peace. I've decided to stay neutral during disputes and stick to facts when raising points and escalating events and requests. If you are planning to leave your soul-sucking organization for peace and productivity, do your homework first. Don't be in such a rush to leave that you jump out of the frying pan and into the fire. Determine the life you want to lead and the type of position you'll need to achieve it. Get granular in detail about your work hours and the environment you'll need that is conducive to your productivity. List everything you'll need to be an employee rock star. Then, apply for positions, interview each person interviewing you, and don't brush away red flags. Money isn't everything.

Lesson 3:
We learn much more through observation than we realize.

Going natural has been a life lesson in how my elders and ancestors saw themselves and me. I'm still learning daily how

Dream Aloud!

small nuances shape our thinking and the way we see ourselves and others.

When I was growing up, little girls didn't get perms that relaxed the natural curl of their African hair. My first recollection of hair is from the early '70s. My mom had an afro, and I wanted one, too, but little girls didn't get their hair cut into styles back then. Now we all know that while the law of what "little girls didn't" do was the law in my house and many homes of the people in my village, it was not the same in other houses. We wore plaited and twisted ponytails gathered at the scalp with barrettes. For special occasions like Easter, a press-and-curl was considered appropriate. The night before church service, little Black girls around the U.S. sat in kitchens with towels around their shoulders and freshly washed and blow-dried hair, awaiting the hot comb and curling iron heated on the stove to reach the proper temperature for straightening hair to the everyday style of most of our mothers before and after the afro revolution period.

You could feel the heat on your skin as mothers ran the smoking comb through sections of hair, careful to "press" each section, including every tiny piece of curl around the hairline because "edges" were supposed to lay down. They would especially focus on the hair at the nape of your neck, which they called "the kitchen" because certain textured hair rolled up like peas in the back. That's the softest, wavy part of my hair, but I still know where the kitchen is because it was a regular topic in Black spaces.

I got my first perm in the form of a Jheri curl at twelve years old. With a Jheri curl, the hair was rod-set with chemicals that loosened tight natural curl patterns to create bouncy curls, sprayed with a smell-good fragrance called curl activator. We all looked like the people we knew who had what we called "good hair." Good hair blew in the wind and didn't need pressed edges or worry about a kitchen, or at least that's what I thought. Good hair looked amazing when we moved from Jheri curls to relaxers that made it silky smooth.

Chemically relaxed hair was most popular when I entered the workforce in the 1990s and was welcomed in office spaces because it was akin to European styles. Braids, locs, and natural styles presented problems for many.

I'd get silky hair, ten inches to be exact, and sit for twelve hours to have my hair braided. Afterward, I wouldn't have to worry about styling it for six weeks. Sometimes, the braids would be so tight that I'd look like I had a stiff neck for the first two days, unable to turn my head without pain. It was the price to pay for beauty, but by whose standards? It wasn't until I went natural that I had to confront the power of tradition, dominant culture, and the various ways it had shaped me.

Mister Charlie don't want to give you a job anyway.
Dress the part.
Speak the part.
Be twice as good.
You can't do what they do.

Although the words were not spoken as much as taught, we got the message. We believe them wholeheartedly and have learned to tap dance, causing burnout. If it's not burnout, then impostor syndrome and many other isms oppress us so that we have no idea of the weight we are under until the burden is lifted.

Dream Aloud!

Lesson 4:
Where there's a will, there's a way.

Indeed, the stories I've told are disheartening and commonplace for Black women in the industry, but plenty of places will honor your expertise and pay you handsomely for it. We just have to get out of our own way.

I stayed too long in an institution that would never change because I thought there was no better way. Perhaps, for a short time, it was the best way, as I didn't have to pay for my son's degree since it was free as long as I was employed there. However, the question is: were the golden handcuffs worth the time I stayed before he entered college and then remained after he entered college? And with student loans now being forgiven, I ask myself if my tap dance was in vain.

I watched people come and go from the university and come back again because it was easier than working at banks and other places that demanded your time 24/7 for the same type of technology work. Just like I found a way to buy a house and fund all the activities my son wanted to do, I found a way to make a different job work, but it didn't hurt bad enough until the last four years or so. During that time, I began trying new things and going back to my days of doing what had to be done to get to the next level while teaching and creating classes for higher education. *Who do you think you are? And how do you think this is going to be good?* asked the voices in my head, but I didn't give up on myself. I kept moving forward. Life got better when I decided I would find a way to press through until I could leave.

"Who are your friends here?" Shirley asked me one day at work. I had no friends who could speak my name in the rooms.

She used the word friends, but she meant supporters. It was her gentle nudge to say, *I know you're well, and I know what's happening here, but there is no one who can speak up for you when you are unable to speak for yourself.* Moving forward, I will not take a job that shows evidence that I will have to fend for myself—a job where I won't have the proper support and sponsorship required to have fair evaluations. I want to work where I am praised for what I do well and supported in the areas where I need improvement. Because there's always a need for improvement. Now, when I think about whose shoulders I stand on, my mother didn't have it as good as I did in employment, but in her papers, I found that she had filed a grievance for promotions she had been passed up for, even though she was well-qualified. She never told me about this, though.

I am sure my grandmother's life did not provide as many choices and luxuries as my mother and I have had, but I am grateful for the sacrifices she made and the sacrifices her mother made for her and her mother before her. Because of their sacrifices, I can hold space where I know I belong and leave spaces where I belong but am not valued.

Lesson 5:
A great title and pay don't mean happiness.

What is happiness, and is there a difference between happiness and joy? We've been taught in church that joy is the thing you want. Joy is the thing you can have even when things aren't going your way, but happiness is a result of conditions that suit you. I believe you can experience happiness even when some conditions aren't good, and joy is something we can

Dream Aloud!

choose to have every day in alignment with gratitude. I think of joy as that which puts a song in my heart. When I ask what makes your heart sing, I'm really asking what brings you joy. Happiness is the overflow of joy that accompanies our emotions and excitement. We can have both when we dare to stop pursuing the status quo definition of success and follow our passions and purpose.

So, these days, I ask myself, *What would I do and still find joy if I weren't getting paid?*

It always goes back to encouraging people with stories, helping them plan to reach their goals, and reminding them who they are so they can have a better life than they ever dreamed of while holding space for their children to live freely in their dream life without regret. If your position causes you to cry every night, gain weight, stress excessively, experience heart palpitations, high blood pressure, and/or lose your hair, it is costing you too much. If you have nice things, such as a car and a house, but you don't have time to spend with your family, it is costing you too much. If you work day in and day out just to have a life on the weekends, then perhaps what you have right now costs too much.

Endless Possibilities

If You're Wondering If Life Has More to Offer, It Does.
~ Steve Harvey

You would not be reading this book if you were not curious about experiencing more in life than you already have. If you're asking, "Is this it?" or if you have checked off your major life goals and now feel that there surely must be something more, that is your soul prompting you. The real you, at the core of your being (which I call your soul), knows your original assignment for every season on this earth, your purpose, and what brings you pure joy. Your purpose never changes, but there are different assignments in various seasons. As a young mother, my assignment was to nurture and develop my son to answer his call. Fulfilling it prepared me to coach and mentor interns and direct reports in my leadership roles with my employer as well as clients and staff in my businesses. There are people attached to your assignment waiting for you to answer your soul's call so they can live out their purpose. If Maya Angelou had not answered the call, what examples would multi-talented, single teen moms with altered paths have to follow? How many more women would have given up before accomplishing their dreams because they thought they were impossible?

While you're out making a life for yourself, you can be sure someone else is watching.

It's not your job to convince everyone that they can do and have what's in their hearts. It's your job to go after everything in your heart. The people assigned to your sphere of influence will notice, draw strength and parallels for their lives, and inspire others just by living.

When I was younger, I watched my cousin go from being a single mother of one to a married and then divorced mother of three, pack her children up, and drive across the country over three days to return to her parents' home. After a few years of working and saving, she testified about moving from a room to her own house. She's been a true example of how life goes on, and you can enjoy it even after what you planned has gone awry. She had no idea I was watching, but I saw her strength and

Dream Aloud!

courage and figured if she could do it with three kids, I could surely do it with just one. Now, if I could only figure out how to look as fabulous as she does when I'm knocking on the door of seventy years old.

    Your turn. Pick out how answering your true calling opens the door for others to live their dreams.

Kendra Newman

Writing Prompt:
My purpose and current assignments are...

Dream Aloud!

Writing Prompt:
Things about my purpose and current assignment that are unclear right now are...

(At this time, you don't have to have the solution to what's unclear after you write them down. You just need to identify them.)

Designing A Life and Livelihood of Impact with The 3L Jumpoff Methodology

Intentional Living Blueprint: Designing a Life of Meaning and Impact.

Now we're at the part of this book you purchased it for—to learn how to create a livelihood that will allow you to live your dreams. One might think we would start by focusing on your skills and which paths to compensation require your abilities. While that is a path to getting paid, it does not necessarily lead to a purpose-driven livelihood that complements your dreams. My tried-and-true 3L Compass Methodology is designed to help you find the intersection of what you're trained to do and what you love to do at the highest compensation rate, providing a lifestyle you've only dreamed of until now.

While working through this methodology, keep in mind that the life of your dreams may be different from what the status quo tells us we should all want. Celebrity life may not be what you want. I, for one, like going to the grocery store and other public places without being recognized. Have you ever heard a celebrity say they miss being able to go out to eat without the paparazzi chasing them down? Some of us want that life, but it's not for everyone.

Maybe you've climbed the corporate ladder and found out it wasn't all it was cracked up to be once you reached the top. Or perhaps you've enjoyed the climb while helping to make your employer a huge success and are ready to do something for yourself now. Either way, you must get clear on a few things before making a plan to live the next chapter of your life in an impactful and meaningful way.

The 3Ls in the methodology stand for Lifestyle, Legacy, and Livelihood. From this point on, we will need to think of them in that order. The methodology leads with lifestyle because it is the manner in which we live. All too often, we allow our means of living to determine the lifestyle we can have.

Imagine creating a living that supports the lifestyle of your dreams. Now, imagine doing something you love to support that lifestyle. The goal is to create a lifestyle-driven livelihood that will leave a legacy you can be proud of, inspire others, and help future generations. Write down the following and place it somewhere you can see it daily.

Lifestyle - *The way we live (a.k.a. the manner in which we live).*
Legacy - *The story of how we have lived.*
Livelihood - *The means by which we earn a living.*

Dream Aloud!

HOW DID I GET HERE?

That is the question most multi-talented professionals with the entrepreneurial trait buried within ask themselves. You've followed the rules, earned the certifications and degrees, landed the job, worked hard, and now you're making a decent living. Your daily routine is solid, and you feel blessed.

What happens when you've reached your career goals and find that it's not all it's cracked up to be? Your job and title look good on the outside; family and community members look up to you. You want more, though, and they can't understand why. After all, you've done so much more than they ever thought of doing, and in some cases, much more than you thought you could accomplish.

While some of the work was hard and required plenty of sacrifice, you know you're coasting for the most part. It's a good gig with great benefits and weekends and holidays off. It's why I chose public service, the non-corporate route—so I could make a difference and have a life. Sound familiar? Is that you, too? Unbeknownst to us, the non-corporate career track has its tap dancing and is chock-full of those people I call corporate failures. Corporate failures want to make a name for themselves in shallow waters and create toxic work environments that turn employees who love their jobs into *go-along-to-get-alongs*, *the disenchanted*, and *coasters* that fill the office.

Lower wages than those offered by corporations were the tradeoff you chose for insane work hours and the bottom line as the sole focus. Non-corporate jobs provide more time to have a personal life. The secret is that it's always about the bottom line, corporate or not. This space is not what you thought it would be. You've spent ten, twenty, or thirty years doing this work—work you can do in your sleep. What should you do now? Use the lessons and skills you've learned in your journey to build your empire!

You've had the opportunity to experience the good, the bad, and the ugly sides of working for your employer, and none of it has to go to waste. Your experience is transferable. Opportunity awaits those who dare to PIVOT and PARLAY the lessons they have learned and the skills they have earned. Life is good, but you must make some moves if you want it to be amazing. I DARE YOU TO BET ON YOU!

I was forty-five when I hit send with my resignation attached to the email address of the Associate Dean of Finance under whom I had worked for three LONG years. She was the last pick of all the interviewees in a group of four candidates, three of whom were more qualified than she was. I understand word came from up high that she would be the pick anyway. The environment was toxic on its own, and turnover from leadership to rank-and-file positions was the norm in the organization long before she signed on. Almost every leader fell into the toxic mold. They seemed to have promising ways at the beginning but, within weeks, would fall into roles that perpetuated the hostile organizational culture or planned and executed their escape quickly, leaving us in the same condition we were in before they arrived.

Perhaps it was the proverbial mold of the organization that contaminated everyone in their seats of authority. Many played along to get along because they had families to feed. Others were just asses, in my opinion—those who couldn't make it in corporate and brought their mischievous ways to public service. No matter the cause, we all suffered.

I'd been in higher education for nineteen years. It was a

Dream Aloud!

wonderful environment for the single mother that I was back when I began as a network operations specialist at age twenty-six. Before that, I worked as a contractor for the city's IT department. As the IT support person, I got to work with every department, and most people I worked with thought I was a city government employee. I was off when they were off (weekends and holidays) and received awards as a bona fide employee. I learned quickly that this was the kind of work environment that suited me, but I didn't want to move into the urban area, which was a requirement to be a full-time employee.

I spent one and a half years as a contractor, having a ball touching every area I studied during my four years of earning my degree in Telecommunications Management and more. I was the network administrator and technology instructor and handled contractor coordination and supervision. I set up computers, printers, and new phones, vetted new software, and spent countless hours under desks and on top of them running coaxial cable through drop ceilings. I was not pleased with my $1,000 raise for doing such a good job, which bumped me to a $26,000 annual salary, but I kept working. My bosses raved about how well I represented the company and how valued I was by them and the city. However, I knew my salary would at least double if I were a city employee. On top of that, I saw a bill from my company on the CIO's desk. The company contracted with the city to provide software engineering support (my title) charged them a whopping $230,000 for the quarter. The itemized details included network support, training, software installation, hardware setup, and telephony. All the line items were pulled from the summary of my weekly accomplishments that I had sent to my supervisor.

103

It was then that I decided I needed to cash in on my expertise. Surely, my company had. Annual raises of $1,000 were the vision of review for my company, and they were far below what I was worth.

My first PIVOT and PARLAY was strategic. I had hands-on experience in multiple technology areas. But honestly, I hated talking about computers. Fixing them, different makes and models—anything related to desktop installation and repair became monotonous, and I didn't want to talk shop at lunch or at home. I wanted to do something more meaningful. I began thinking about how my next job would support what I wanted for my life.

- I wanted a master's degree and a Ph.D. without more student loans. (At my low salary, that $289/month loan repayment was hurting a sistah.)
- I wanted the same work hours and weekends and holidays off as I had while working for the city.
- Great health benefits were a must.
- I wanted to be a professor at a university by the age of thirty.
- I wanted to be an example to my son that you can go after your dreams.
- Lastly, I wanted to spend time with my son because I realized there are no do-overs when raising children. If you miss something, you can never get that time back.

I applied to a university in the city and a startup data management company closer to my house. The data management company called first, offering $24,000 and travel reimbursement. When I talked to my father about it, he was

Dream Aloud!

pleased and told me that taking the position would be good. The job was up the street, so I would save money on gas and tolls.

With hesitation, I turned down the job. I wanted to learn more about databases and give myself another layer of skills I didn't have. However, I had a gnawing feeling I would end up calling the director—as I had for the MCI telephony position I'd accepted earlier in northern New Jersey—to tell him that I had to back out of the offer, which paid fifty percent more than the contracting position I had. When my dad asked me why, I told him God had something better for me. I had already worried him because I was a part of this Word of Faith church that spoke in tongues, praised in dance, and occasionally ran around the sanctuary. We believed in manifested healing and that anything that happened in the Bible could and should happen now as daily-life occurrences.

It wasn't so much me that he was worried about, but rather his grandson who spewed The Word in daily conversation with conviction and knowing. My dad would repeatedly say to me, "I have never seen someone… (insert whatever my son told him he was believing for)." My response was, "Just because you haven't seen it doesn't make it any less true." Approximately three months after I turned down that database management position, the university called and presented an offer of $32,000. I now know that I should have negotiated for a higher starting salary, but it was more money than I had ever made. When I told my dad, his only response was, "Praise the Lord!"

I've used my pivot and parlay process to earn extra income teaching what I know as an independent contractor and adjunct professor, doing what I love in my travel agency, strategic and event planning, switching roles between employee and employer, providing Lifestyle, Legacy, and Livelihood-based coaching services, and giving back through my community learning initiative.

While I'd been working on leveraging my experience to create multiple income streams, I was also volunteering for projects that interested me. I took on various roles that made me a viable independent contractor and adjunct professor, working on my own terms. I had many technology skills but little business and leadership experience outside of managing contractors. My pivot and parlay process is tried and proven not only by me but also by my clients. Meet Sharron, a successful corporate leader who wanted to fulfill her dreams of running her own company. She had started and stopped pursuing her dreams of running her athletic wear company many times, wondering if she should wait until retirement to go hard in her business and worried that it was too late to start in her late 50s. Besides, she made good money and would be financially okay now and in the future if she kept plugging away at her 9-to-5.

After committing to my Live Your Dreams! 8-week private Jumpstart Program (which is jam-packed with processes like Parlay and Pivot to give my clients the edge they need to produce results quickly), Sharron got clear about what she truly wanted in every area of her life. She became serious about creating the soul-satisfying lifestyle she envisioned and stepped into her authority as CEO of Inside Out Athletic Wear LLC. Sharron made her first sale four months earlier than planned, giving her the momentum to advance in her entrepreneurial journey and grow her business. She has since beefed up her plan for her upcoming collection, strengthened her social media presence, and undergone a personal transformation that began with one round of pivot and parlay action.

Then there's Kim, who had been "laid off" from her job as a

Dream Aloud!

social worker during the start of the COVID-19 pandemic. She was the go-to person in her office and a threat to insecure managers who didn't see themselves as adequate in their leadership positions. I say she was released to her destiny. She says she was fired. Either way, she decided she would work for herself. She had her real estate license and was certified as a notary, and just like at work, she was the go-to person for family, friends, and community members to help buy and sell houses, notarize documents, and draw up contracts.

Using the Pivot and Parlay process, Kim smashed her twelve-month income goals during the height of the pandemic in the first quarter of the year! She has now parlayed her skill set and pivoted into an additional income stream that complements her real estate and signing agent work.

"Change will not come if we wait for some other person or if we wait for some other time. We are the ones we've been waiting for. We are the change that we seek."
~ Lurie Daniel Favors

Remember my goals when I was looking for a university position? I also created a plan to achieve them. Please note that a plan is only as good as we are. We must be flexible and able to quickly abandon what does not work or no longer serves us. We can plan for many things, but there are some life events that we just cannot foresee. If we had known about the 9/11 terrorist attacks, the 2008 housing bust, and the pandemic of 2020 before their occurrences, how different would our plans for life, love, and career have been? How much were we required to pivot because of those three events alone?

While I was successful in accomplishing some goals—like

increasing my salary while maintaining a great schedule, getting my second degree nearly free of charge, earning plenty of certifications, enjoying great health benefits, and being presented with opportunities to write my ticket as an independent contractor because of my new skill set, I made significant pivots.

After a few years, I no longer wanted to be a professor; the political landscape was not my cup of tea. I thought I wanted a Ph.D. in research until I learned that the goal was really about making money, not making a difference. In most cases, it was a popularity contest, and members of the surrounding communities were the guinea pigs they needed to obtain more grants. However, they looked different from the students they recruited for the schools and colleges that ran the clinics, which enticed families with trials that paid stipends. I began to shift how I could make a difference in my community without the tap dancing I saw well-meaning faculty jig through daily.

Plans are made to be adjusted and readjusted as you learn more about who you are meant to be and what you want. You have the right to change your mind. Need to make a pivot? Just do it.

Dream Aloud!

What's going well for you right now?

_____
_____
_____
_____
_____
_____
_____
_____

What needs to change?

_____
_____
_____
_____
_____
_____
_____
_____
_____
_____

The Pivot and Parlay Process

Pivot (verb) - *to turn on a point.*

Pivot is also a noun—a central point (pin, shaft, or similar) on which a mechanism turns. Think of the noun as your point of reference and the verb as the turn you need to make to change your situation. The Pivot and Parlay process assumes you will make a controlled turn toward your goal. It can be the slightest degree or a complete 180-degree turn.

Parlay (verb) – *to turn earnings from a previous bet into higher stakes. As a noun, parlay means an accumulation of winnings from a bet.*

Perhaps you've taken the job you're currently in to make ends meet as a stepping stone to do what you love later. Or maybe the plan was to do what you love on the side, or you desire to retire from your current job before starting another income stream to supplement your pension and Social Security (assuming you live in the United States). I suggest trying some of the things you love before leaving your 9-to-5. Your hobby can become a lucrative business if you apply your experience and talents with the intention of turning it into a new stream of income for yourself. If you've determined you need to pivot, I suggest you start with the MY PIVOT AND PARLAY PROCESS.

Step 1: Choose your path.
Step 2: Take inventory of your parlay.
Step 3: Create opportunity.
Step 4: Pivot as necessary.
Step 5: Repeat.

Your parlay is the sum of your experience. You will leverage this to gain even more experience, which will provide you with the credentials you need to take advantage of opportunities and make various choices.

Let's go back to my client, Kim. Once her employer released her to her destiny, she needed to take a step back, choose her next steps (Pivot & Parlay Step 1), and reevaluate the contents of her Experience Toolbox (Step 2) based on her choice. Remember the saying, "Beggars can't be choosers"? While this is true for beggars, you must first decide who you are. Are you a beggar? If so, you don't have the luxury of choosing much of what you want for yourself. The good news is that you can

Dream Aloud!

choose not to be a beggar. You don't have to stay where you are. Good choices lead to better choices, often with variety.

If I walk into a Louis Vuitton store with a thousand dollars, I'm not one of the shoppers who doesn't have to ask how much an item is before I purchase it because I am limited to what my thousand dollars can buy. I am in the category "If you have to ask, you probably can't afford it." My choices are limited to lower-ticket items. I can create an opportunity for myself to have more options to purchase if I shop when Louis Vuitton is having a sale. I can increase the odds of buying something I want if I show up early and get my hands on what's available before other bargain shoppers arrive.

Kim made a choice NOT to work for anyone else and, by default, chose to work for herself. She created opportunities for herself using her experience (Step 3). She'd been selling homes in her spare time and decided to make that her primary source of income during the pandemic. There was an associated skill that she parlayed into the new livelihood she was designing for herself. She parlayed her notary credentials into becoming a signing agent to take advantage of the great income opportunities that accompanied purchasing or refinancing a home. Kim has created opportunities to receive income from selling homes and for helping others who were not her real estate clients to close on their mortgages.

You want to be ready whenever opportunity knocks. Initially, Kim was preparing to double down on her real estate career, but interest rates were so low at the height of the pandemic that she made an unexpected majority of her income from homeowners taking advantage of the low rates. She didn't have to get ready; she already was and cashed in while refinancing was hot. Knowing that it would not last forever, she switched from the brokerage firm that knew her as a part-time agent to one that saw her as the badass sales agent she already was.

Now that interest rates have climbed, she is focusing more on home sales as she has less than half the signings she did in 2020 and 2021 (Step 4). She's not stuck in an interest rate hike or home refinancing lull; more people are still looking for housing than there are available. This means home prices will be higher, and her agent's pay will be higher. Don't think she stopped there. Kim is working on new streams of income using many of her existing skills and talents, which will create a new set of choices and paths to follow (Step 5).

"Opportunities of a lifetime must be seized in the lifetime of the opportunity."

~ Linda Ravenhill

What opportunities are you able to create for yourself right now? How will these opportunities create more choices for you? What is your Pivot & Parlay strategy?

Step 1: Choose your path — What do you want for your lifestyle and legacy, and what will you do to create your unique livelihood to support it?

Step 2: Take inventory of your parlay — Identify your transferable skills and experiences to begin generating income on your new path.

Step 3: Create opportunity — Opportunity is all around you. What can you do right now to create opportunities?

Dream Aloud!

Step 4: Pivot as necessary — Be willing to change quickly as necessary, whether with a little tweak or a complete about-face.

Step 5: Repeat — You never arrive at your goal destination to stay. You enjoy it for a while, and then it's on to better things. You'll know when it's time.

How will you know when it's time to pivot? When your comfort zone becomes uncomfortable. If you're uncomfortable where you are, it's time to make a move. Nothing grows in the comfort zone. That's why you're starting to wonder if there's more out there. Each time you consider stepping out, your mind begins asking, "What if?"

What if...I leave this company and can't find anything else?
What if...I'm wrong?
What if...I lose money?
What if...they think I'm crazy? (Who are "they" anyway?)

When we don't move, what-ifs turn into "I should have," "I could have," and "I wish." I call this the "Shoulda, Coulda, Woulda" Club.

Most people won't pivot until the pain of remaining the same becomes too much for them. I could have left my job after the first dean and boss trauma, but I stayed until I gained twenty pounds, my hair fell out, and I was working almost 24/7 for a total of four executive leaders, hoping the environment would change.

Is this you? Ask yourself if you are really stuck or just choosing to stay. You think about moving on, but you're telling yourself you are comfortable where you are. But are you? The very fact that you're thinking about making changes indicates that you are no longer comfortable. The thing that you feel is SAFE is not entirely safe. It's a sense of safety that is weighed down by the fear of the unknown. We spend so much time playing it safe that we may never know all the opportunities we've missed simply because we were afraid or unwilling to take risks.

You can have your cake and eat it, too, meaning you can keep your day job and take steps to venture into some new income-generating areas that are new to you. What do you have to lose? The risks are probably pride—if it doesn't go well—and non-support from family and friends who may not see your vision. But how will you know if what you're contemplating is really what you want if you don't try it? It's well worth the energy.

JUST BECAUSE YOU CAN DO IT DOESN'T MEAN YOU SHOULD.

Remember when I first started in tech, setting up and troubleshooting desktop computer problems? While I'm good at it, I don't particularly enjoy it. After a day of people tugging and pulling at me to solve their problems, I would find myself exhausted and irritable, trying my best not to come off as the Computer Guy on SNL. (Look him up. It was hilariously accurate for techs in the early personal computing days.) Too many of us work in environments we don't love or that bring us very little joy because the money and benefits are good. Or worse, we do it because we feel that saying no to such an opportunity is being ungrateful. We multi-talented folks are good at many things, but that doesn't mean we should make it our life's work. It doesn't matter how impressive the title is, how high a pedestal family and friends put you on for doing it, or the size of the check that comes with it. No amount of money or prestige can save our mental, physical, or spiritual health when a soul-sucking responsibility is our vehicle for making a living.

DOES IT FIT MY LIFESTYLE?

I remind my clients that they are royalty and should treat themselves as such. They are also encouraged to take charge of their lives and livelihoods as CEOs (Chief Executive Officers), improving their lives one executive decision at a time. Every royal CEO should interview herself. Remember the MCI position I turned down before I took the contracted position? Why would someone straight out of college turn down a $38,000 entry-level position at one of the world's three largest Baby Bell companies in 1995? Raising my child in a safe environment surrounded by people I loved was more important than working the night shift and leaving him with strangers. That job was located in West Orange, New Jersey. I was sure I couldn't afford rent in West Orange, which meant renting in Orange, Maplewood—if I were lucky—and possibly Newark. Not such great places for a single mom to raise a Black boy and be away from home in the evening.

So many single mothers have to spend time making ends meet that they don't get to spend quality time with their children. Unwilling to accept that as my fate, I moved home to South Jersey, where the cost of living was lower. I worked in a city in the next state over to earn more than I could anywhere within thirty miles of my house, except for the Atlantic City casinos, which required some holidays, weekends, and possibly nights in the tech world. This pivot fit my lifestyle and the non-negotiable parenting goals I had set. I wanted to be able to say I had done everything in my power to raise a good, productive citizen without regret.

Some goals are negotiable, but the ones that are not should never be removed from your plan. You build a strategy to pivot in ways that allow you to still hit the non-negotiables on your list.

Align your PIVOT and PARLAY STRATEGY with the season you are in. My pivot into higher ed was the beginning of my life's summer. I was a young, single mom with a degree that could open many doors, determining my career path and the life I wanted for my child. My pivot into leadership was closing my summer season. Now, in the autumn of life, I'm enjoying the warmth of "Indian Summers" and looking forward to the colorful landscapes of changing leaves. I could have stayed in what was thought to be my safe space, but each time I stretched, I built my parlay.

When I was squeezed to my wit's end, never feeling one hundred percent healthy, losing hair, and gaining weight, I had to make a choice. After nineteen years of employment, I was part of the fabric, but I knew that if I could leave the unit under which I was oppressed, I would be better off. The life I had dreamed of included attending the organization's twenty-year club. I also looked forward to having the phenomenal health care provided to all employees in retirement.

I did not have to worry about the pension plan because, during the onboarding session, we were all steered away from what I now know was the pension being offered. The HR leadership that ran the orientation had vaguely told us it was going away. Ignorance is costly, but it can work out for your

Dream Aloud!

good even when you make mistakes. If I'd had the "good" pension plan, I most likely would have stayed until I was fired or in bad health. Since I had nothing to lose and increased pay, which equals increased retirement contributions at my new job, I didn't have to consider remaining in such a toxic environment. Preparing for winter, I want to enjoy the fruits of my labor and not burden my family.

What season are you in? Knowing that life is short, no matter how long you live, it's time to get busy living on your terms.

Write down your vision for yourself for the season you're currently in. Be sure to explain the feelings you want to experience while living your vision.

_____
_____
_____
_____
_____
_____
_____
_____
_____
_____
_____
_____

Kendra Newman

Dream Aloud!

SHAPE YOUR IDENTITY

I AM. The two most powerful words you will ever speak are I AM. Be careful what you say after I AM, though. Remember, your mind is trained to believe whatever you think about yourself. Therefore, your daily mantras should reinforce the life that you want. Use the vision you wrote about your season to create "I AM" mantras that uplift and shift your mind's perspective to promote everything you want for your life.

I AM…healthy.
I AM…content.
I AM…loved.

Now, write everything you are on paper and hang it somewhere you will see it daily. SPEAK THE WORDS ALOUD daily to shape your identity for the new level you are moving to in your life.

THE UNAPPROACH

What do you do when you've dreamed of and manifested a position but don't want it?

To paraphrase Lindsay Fauntleroy's (author of *In Our Element: Using the Five Elements as Soul Medicine to Unleash Your Personal Power*) answer to a similar question on what to do when you get what you THOUGHT you wanted during an interview: "There are soul lessons. You are precious. Your time and intelligence are precious. You have the right and authority to move outside of what you've manifested. Just because you've manifested it doesn't mean your divinity requires you to sit in it. Everything is subject to death and decay; it's temporal. The reason you are being called to let something go is because you are feeling grief. Grief that this is not what you wanted or hoped for. Reflect and acknowledge what needs to be let go to start something new. This is dying. This hurts, and it's painful, but it must happen.

If something is not working for the collective, it's probably not working for the individuals. If you are the sole person holding up something that is destined to fall apart, it's for naught. Why are you putting more resources into something that is dying? You don't have to hold it together. Step out and let destiny.

I'm better than this (but I've done it). You don't have to sit in the seat you've made for yourself if you no longer wish to do so."

There is nothing new under the sun. Moving forward can bring grief. Follow Lindsay Fauntleroy's advice, and don't let emotions get stuck and crystallize in your body. Get unstuck with the unapproach. It's been designed by yours truly to help you advance with your hopes and dreams when you know all that you've been taught and are accustomed to is holding you back. Use the checklist provided to start undoing everything that no longer serves you.

Dream Aloud!

UNAPPROACH QUICK CHECKLIST

- **Change Your Thoughts and Create New Worlds of Reality**

- **Write It, Say It, Visualize It**

- **Use Mantras**
  Don't just say it; living it is better.

- **Sometimes, Our Solutions Are Things We've Already Done**
  Just because it didn't work before doesn't mean it won't work now.

- **Learn Something New Often**
  I believe in forward movement and learning new beneficial things, but we are often too quick to adopt the new and forget good things.

- **Create Your Own**
  When we were a segregated nation, there were Black hospitals, banks, theaters, churches, doctors, nurses, business owners, etc., and we thrived. Who's to say you can't be the catalyst for the next wave? This has nothing to do with just doing business with people who look like you but everything to do with using this example to do business and work with people who think like you in the areas of hiring and promoting based on merit instead of preference.

- **Move When Prompted**
  The feeling you have to take action on something is not to be ignored, reasoned away, or vetted by anyone else but you.

MOVE WHEN PROMPTED

You don't have to know the whole story. Just move, and the big picture will come into focus at the right time.

My entire life has been shaped by promptings and the consequences of following them or not. I was prompted not to give my phone number to the beautiful guy on the other side of the concession stand where I worked at the racetrack. After much begging and conceding, I found myself in a relationship with an abusive narcissist who wanted to control my entire life and abandoned the child he cried for when I walked away from the relationship.

I was prompted to attend a degree-granting trade school as a 19-year-old single mother to get my bachelor's degree in engineering. In the middle of my third semester of school, I switched my major from engineering to telecommunications management. I knew engineers made a lot of money, and I could do the job. However, I didn't find building circuits exciting and wanted to be around people. Who knew my telecommunications career would be the best foundation I needed to become the Pivot and Parlay Empress I am today? GOD DID! That one prompt has royally set me up to assume IT director roles, manage projects, design applications, and teach everything I know in meaningful ways. We'll talk about that later.

Mid-career story: I was transitioning from hands-on technology specialist work to technology project management.

Dream Aloud!

I worked on both sides of the coin—a little application building and plenty of technology planning for functional departments that needed guidance on automating their office processes. My job was to observe their day-to-day operations and propose ways to make their processes more efficient using technology. I also participated in many enterprise-wide IT projects, from changing email platforms to large collaboration applications. I served as an instructor of technology, teaching members of our organization how to use various software packages, and I created some of the seminars myself. When it came to performance, I received good reviews and a measly 3% increase when I was sure others were getting more. I'd asked about a true raise. I had trained everyone in the Network Operations Center before leaving to pursue a technology planning career and my passion for project management. It seemed everyone I had trained and educated about project management standards was being promoted, but I wasn't. I scheduled a meeting with my director and asked what I needed to do to get a real raise since the assistant director I reported to directly told me it was in the director's hands to promote.

My department director told me I needed to be assigned more visible projects because the vice president was the true approver of promotions. Was it that they had found no real justification for my promotion from my long list of presidential initiatives, training courses I created, the success of coworkers who had trained under me, and the new skills I had acquired and shared with my group? Or did they just not think I was worthy of a promotion? Thus began the jumping through hoops and the dangling of carrots.

I asked them to explain why my list of accomplishments was not promotion-worthy. When they could not provide a good reason for this, I was told I needed a master's degree. I had already been working toward my MBA with a concentration in Project Management. Six months later, I showed up for another meeting with my Master of Project Management in hand. The new excuse was that there was no money at the time, and they would get back to me. Every six weeks, I would ask for a meeting until the assistant director, to whom I reported directly, told me that to get promoted, I would need to obtain my Project Management Professional certification. I had heard it was a difficult test, and before completing my degree, I had been looking at all the requirements to become certified. I ended up deciding that a master's in the subject should suffice. I protested that I'd just gotten a master's degree in the very subject at their direction, to which he replied, "Yes, but the PMP holds more weight for the promotion you are trying to get." I knew this was another hoop to jump through. My guess is that they thought it was something I could not accomplish. They'd been surprised by my master's degree, but they had friends and colleagues they trusted and admired who had failed the PMP exam. Surely, they didn't believe I would pass if those people didn't.

That day, I called a friend who worked for IBM and had recently earned his PMP. He told me about a training company that provided an intensive boot camp for professionals looking to pass the PMP exam on the first try. I thanked him for the information and contacted them immediately for details on determining if I qualified to register.

On my day off, in the middle of the week, I was prompted to complete my department's process of entering a request for a requisition for payment for training. I got the notion to submit my request for the Intensive PMP Exam boot camp in the middle of singing while housecleaning. I immediately stopped mopping

Dream Aloud!

my kitchen floor and logged onto my computer to enter my request so as not to let it slip my mind later in the day. After hitting send, I returned to my kitchen cleaning duties. When I returned to the office two days later, the assistant director approached me, questioning me in a knowing tone.

"You put in a request for a training requisition a few days ago?" he asked.

"Yes," I replied.

He then said, "Next time, you should ask me before submitting a requisition request."

Now listen, I've entered a request for requisition on many occasions, and I've never had to ask for permission to submit a request! The supervisor must approve all requests before they are moved into the purchasing office's queue to create a requisition purchase order.

I suggested he would not approve it if he didn't want me to attend the training, but asking for permission to submit a request for what I wanted was ridiculous. Even though he said he would approve it, he told me to ask next time. My ears perked up at that request. This hoop was meant to be the last barrier they put up, and here I was, jumping through it…again. Later, I learned that the group I had been a member of before joining the one I was in had been fired, and their defense—with the help of labor lawyers—was that they had asked for training and were denied. My timing for entering my request (unaware of the issues unfolding with my former group) was perfect for getting the most crucial training of my career at that time approved. I am sure my requisition would have been denied if the company had not been facing a lawsuit of sorts.

I have many examples of what happens when you follow your heart or spirit's guidance, listen to your gut, and move when prompted; they're all the same action. It simply means you move when the urge to do something arises in your thoughts. At that point, you must decide if you will brush it off because your inner voice says no or because your body is now relaxed and resisting the urge to move. The other choice is to FOLLOW THE PROMPTING.

Following the prompting may not make sense at the time, but trust me, it builds faith. Lives have been saved because of these promptings. How many stories have you heard about someone deciding not to go to work or catch a flight they needed to be on for whatever reason, following their gut, and learning later that if they had brushed off the warning their gut was giving them, however slight, they would have been in a terrible accident or even lost their life?

Hindsight is 20/20, but visibility may be zero at the time of the prompting. It takes practice to let your heart work in conjunction with your head and body to achieve success in areas where you had no clue an opportunity or roadblock awaited. I liken it to driving through foggy patches. Visibility can be low as you move through the patch. Not knowing what's on the other side, you slow down to be able to brake in case of an emergency and hope that oncoming traffic has its headlights on.

Signs That You Need to Create Your Exit Strategy Now

"Hold on," I told myself while holding my face like flint, my head held high on my way to my office. The minute the door closed behind me, I locked it and fell into the chair behind my desk as the tears began to flow. I was quiet so no one would hear me. I felt hopeless and helpless. What more could I do? I was in charge of virtual and on-premise classroom and laboratory technology integration and support, spread over three campuses and multiple buildings for eight units under the purview of one college within my university. My portfolio also included research and administrative support, website administration, privacy and security management, research and development, disaster recovery planning, training, and any other duties assumed to be those of the IT Director.

We were always short-staffed, and for over a year, I was the only in-house IT employee, rolling up my sleeves to take care of as many duties as possible while relying on the university's central IT desktop and networking partners to help me. It was during this time that my boss gave me a midterm review that I interpreted as *You suck. You have no skills, and the department chairs and staff hate you.* I was tired of defending myself and explaining that we needed more people. I would arrive at 7 AM to complete my administrative work and be ready for the onslaught of classroom and desktop support requests that would begin at 9 AM. Then, I would go on until 4 PM or later, only to stay another 3-4 hours to work on the website and ensure everything was set up for events planned for the next day.

I worked hard to get to this position. When I graduated from college with my Bachelor of Telecommunications Management degree, I was ready to take on the world. My first job title was Software Engineer at a small technology firm contracted by the City of Philadelphia. I loved the job, and everyone thought I was a city worker. There was more than enough work to keep me busy and learning. Although my overall job description listed only duties associated with desktop application support, I was the IT support for all the departments, providing networking (my formal training area), training, and managing staff from subcontractors.

Dream Aloud!

YOU NEED TO EXECUTE YOUR EXIT STRATEGY IF:
- Your ideas are used, but you don't get credit for them.
- Your CYA efforts keep you up at night replying to email.
- Family time is sacrificed to meet work deadlines, even while on vacation.
- You dread going into the office.
- Alternative facts are the norm for excuses made by those.
- Your mental and physical health is suffering under the weight of organizational pressures.

YOUR EXIT STRATEGY SHOULD INCLUDE:
- Medical Coverage Planning — There may be a gap between when you move on to your second act and when new coverage kicks in. Get all of your physicals, tests, and procedures that you've been putting off done before you move on.
- Financial — Calculate how much you'll need to earn to live the way you want while doing what you love.
- 3L Plan — How do you envision the next level of your lifestyle, legacy, and livelihood? List your non-negotiables and keep them at the forefront of your mind. Assess the realistic value of your skills and how you can use them to live in line with your purpose and passion.

4 WAYS TO CREATE INCOME THAT FITS YOUR LIFESTYLE:
- Get a new job. You'll have a greater ability to negotiate salary, benefits packages, time off, and the location where you wish to live than you do with your current employer.

- Use your transferable skills to become an independent contractor. Help other companies achieve their goals and charge what you're worth.
- Teach what you know. You have the experience and expertise that others need.
- Create your own lifestyle-driven business. Make the contract, set the goals, and build your empire.

We are the sum of our experiences, gifts, and talents. Like my dad, I am good at many things. He has held government jobs, worked in clothing factories, served as the local barber and community BBQ master, prepared taxes for family and friends, been a Sunday school superintendent and teacher, and bartended at various establishments, weddings, and other private events. If he didn't know how to do something, he figured it out and became the go-to guy. By the time I graduated from college, I was a mother, seamstress, bellhop, cook, home DIY enthusiast, project manager, and technology specialist. I've reinvented my title and my world many times. I now know that no experience is ever wasted.

Remember to reinvent your title to satisfy all the dimensions of your being, to accommodate all that you are. We remain who we are at our core. The phrase "reinvent yourself" doesn't sit well with me. It implies that who we are needs to change. Changing who we are at our core to fit into labels and expectations that we have not personally set requires us to be untrue to ourselves.

Many choose to reinvent themselves and abandon their true identity. This is a surface-deep life that leads to unfulfillment and becoming a member of the dreaded "Shoulda, Coulda,

Dream Aloud!

Woulda" club. My goal is to save myself and many others who are willing to live fully from that club of regret. To live your dreams out loud and in color, you must remain who you are at your core. Fight against societal norms by going against the grain; creatively use your gifts and talents in multiple ways to generate income. Find fulfillment in doing the things you love, and leave this world a better place while making an impact on the people in it.

Gifts and talents are discovered through the experience of events. Skills are developed and sharpened, as well. Dare to try new things. Give yourself permission to be a beginner. I know you've been an expert in your field for years, but to find your special niche—a group that needs what you have to offer, specifically from you, you must unlock combinations of skills, hobbies, passions, and purpose. Start by trying new things. Of course, some will not be for you, but you will know when you're onto something your ideal customer wants and makes your heart sing.

Once you get that "heart singing" feeling, you'll never forget it. Make operating in that mode part of your life's mission. It will guide you to move away from what does not serve you—even if it did in the past—and prompt you to move toward whatever awaits you for a better future. There are multiple levels of life. Keep allowing yourself to elevate and experience all that life has to offer.

Go back to the bullet points for this section and determine which of the four ways to create the income you will start working on right now. There's no time like the present. Maybe you plan to do all four, but may I suggest focusing on one at a time? There's no need to do everything right away. However, you must take action on one immediately.

Kendra Newman

HOW TO TELL IF YOU'RE WORKING IN A GOLDEN HANDCUFFS ENVIRONMENT:
- Water cooler talk revolves around retirement countdowns.
- The benefits are good, but the pay is low.
- The pay is good, but time for personal life is almost nonexistent.
- "At least..." consultation statements give the incentive to stay. Examples: "At least I don't have to work weekends." "At least I have summers off." "At least I can afford to take a vacation."

IS THE WRITING ON THE WALL?

Be intentional to read every sign. If the handwriting is on the wall, you're behind the eight ball. Don't wait until you can read the full sign to get a plan. (See the Exit Strategy section of this book.)

We were gathered at a table, shooting the breeze after a meeting. You know, the type of after-meeting, off-topic conversations that include smiles (genuine or otherwise) and people letting down their guard a little. This is the time to pay close attention to what is being said and why. These conversations reveal your company's culture–what your colleagues think of the world, themselves, and you.

Our barely 30-something boss was a type of phoenix. She had shown up in the department, clearly unqualified, with easily detected "fake it 'til you make it" competence, even though everyone was aware of her ability to rise from the ashes of every departmental firebomb explosion she set, leaving calamity and destruction in her wake. When she was hired to lead our college, it was clear that she had been the "project" of someone in executive leadership, even though she ranked fourth out of the four candidates who interviewed to replace the outgoing AVP. In fact, the consensus of the search committee was to choose from the top two candidates, which dwarfed the third and fourth candidate choices. So how did we end up with the fourth-ranked candidate whose experience, skills, and overall qualifications paled in comparison to the third-ranked candidate, who was clearly not closely ranked with the first two? You guessed it. It really is about who you know. Sometimes, knowing the right people can put you in a position to grow and prosper at the risk of hanging whole organizations out to dry.

For some, it's not about the bottom line and productivity as much as it's about helping friends and climbing the ladder. The assumption is that others will pull the weight, or it's more important to LOOK professional than to actually BE able to perform a role. Woe to those of us who have been subjected to "leaders" who aren't qualified in the least to lead themselves. Prepare to suffer the backlash of such a leader's insecurities, bad decisions, false blaming, and downright lies. They have little talent except for surviving the gauntlet of obstacles for which they are unqualified to solve, no matter how many casualties take place. Those types of individuals are in position for one reason—to get to the top by any means necessary.

DON'T BE A CASUALTY. STAY VIGILANT.

Our "casual" after-meeting conversation went something like this. Phoenix asked what everyone was doing for the weekend. The group commented, and then the topic changed to a retirement party. We discussed how promotions in higher education usually come only with someone's retirement (or passing) because it's a good place to work for maintaining work-life balance. The topic then shifted to how long each of us had been employed at the institution, the various roles we've filled, and so on.

That's when Phoenix commented, "Out of all of us, Kendra's been here the longest. Nineteen years is a long time."

My third ear went up. I had never told any of them how long I'd been working for the university. So, clearly, she had done some research on my tenure. I smiled and kept a neutral face, not letting her know I knew she had been checking me out.

You must do several things when you find yourself on the "Check Them Out" list.

One: Why would it be important to know what they've revealed they know?

Thanks to human resource policies, one must have just cause to fire someone. Firing someone for poor performance must come with evidence of previous observations and documentation of inadequate performance, probationary periods, etc. I had none in nineteen years.

Two: How do they know?

Think of where the party must go to get the information they've revealed. In my case, Phoenix would've had to look at my employment records. She could have looked up my HR records to see when I started working at the institution, but my Spidey senses told me that she had consulted with HR to find out how she could rid herself of me and was told there was nothing in my records over the past nineteen years that would warrant such action.

Dream Aloud!

Three: What is going on around you?

Since I had no disciplinary write-ups in my nineteen years of employment at the institution and had worked in various offices and departments, it was clear that I would be a harder target than other employees. At least two of us began receiving email messages in the guise of feedback with subliminal suggestions that we had done things wrong. I was careful to respond to each email, addressing every point of feedback. However, my colleague did not respond and was fired three days after Phoenix told her she was doing a good job.

She had it out for both of us, but my colleague was in her fourth year at the college and did not document everything. I suggested she respond to every received email, follow-up review, and shady comment with a written summary of what was discussed and her responses to any concerns raised. She did not follow my advice and lost her job.

In addition to firings, there will be people who jump ship because they can no longer endure the antagonizing scrutiny of repeatedly proving themselves, while untalented hacks rise to greater positions that require more work from their talented direct reports.

Even though organizations usually have no retaliation policies, retaliation for not "playing along" can occur. Don't wait to become a victim of such actions. When you observe office bullying or any form of punishment, please know that the same can happen to you. You can go from observer to recipient of such treatment at any time because it is often allowed and systemic in business. Get out!

Four: Have they stopped talking to you or inviting you to enterprise meetings about your area of responsibility?

Phoenix and the new dean began meeting with our technology partners without me. I was only told about these meetings when they needed my help to provide an update or an opinion. Wouldn't you think it's odd that decisions that include your department are being made, yet you have no say? That's because they're making moves to do things without you.

There's no need to panic; just prepare for your next move. You're good at what you do. Another organization will value your skill set and provide the environment you need to thrive.

These are the signs that your job is done at your current place of employment and it's time to execute your exit strategy:

- You are no longer included in discussions about areas for which you are responsible.
- What is being done contrasts with what is said about you.
- Your skills are transferable. Leave on your own terms.

Wait, you don't have an exit strategy? Let this be the last day that you have none.

IT'S NOT YOU, IT'S THEM

Sometimes, we're led to believe things that just aren't true. In a short time, you can determine if you're truly not worthy of promotion or if they're saving a position elevation and increase in pay for someone other than you.

Earlier in this chapter, I told my hoops and carrots story.

Dream Aloud!

What's yours? Are you constantly promised a promotion, time off, and more leverage if you complete a task, but after completing the task, you are given excuses for why the promise will not be fulfilled? If this happens multiple times, you are on the hamster wheel. The goal of management is to keep the employee busy with tasks that will take a long time to complete, buying them time to either find money to pay the employee what they're worth or, in many cases, avoid increasing their pay (by assigning goals they believe an employee cannot achieve). When the goal is achieved, the employer finds something else to keep them out of the way for longer. Don't play this game. Move on.

There's always money for the things they want. While they're playing Hoops and Carrots with you, other colleagues are being promoted, new hires are happening, and the office parties are getting more expensive. This is your sign that it's true they don't have the money to increase your salary…BECAUSE THEY DON'T WANT TO INCREASE YOUR SALARY. There is, however, money in the budget for everything they want because they create long-term and short-term budgets for everything they deem appropriate.

If you're more than two years into being added to the budget, chances are there is no money for your salary increase because they don't want what you want. The message could not be any clearer. Move on!

Accepting lower wages than you are worth affects your current lifestyle and, most importantly, your retirement status. Remember, the salary you earn today determines your Social Security, 401(k), and Roth contributions and the yields that will sustain you in retirement. The goal is to be able to live as you wish, not as your fixed income dictates.

Kendra Newman

WHAT TO DO WHEN IT IS YOU, NOT THEM

Okay, let's be honest. Sometimes we are the problem. If that's the case, then own it! Our performance will suffer when life happens to the best of us. We cannot control many circumstances: illness, family issues, and some financial events. When these things happen to us, we must adjust how we approach our work. This could mean working different hours, taking time off, or talking to a supervisor and/or HR. (Make sure you put something in writing to have a timestamp showing when you disclosed your issue to your organization.) What you should not do is pretend that everything is okay. If you are unqualified or overwhelmed by your current position, please, for the love of God, get a mentor and read as much as you can to improve your skill set. Do know that you aren't the first person to bite off more than you could chew at the time, but if you stick with it and dedicate yourself to getting better, you will. Lastly, if you're well physically and mentally, all is well at home, and you're more than qualified (or can do your job with your eyes closed) but just don't want to do the work…THEN IT'S TIME TO GET THE HELL OUT OF THERE!

If any of these are your case, my advice is to begin executing your exit strategy. If you are not, your soul is definitely suffering. Pull out that exit plan that details the roadmap to the work that leads to the life you want and make it happen! YOU AREN'T PERFECT. ASSESS, APPROVE, AND MOVE ON.

Not only are you not perfect, but you never need to be. You just need to do your best. Take out your job description and review what you do well and what you aren't doing well. Ask yourself why. Then think about your work—what you were born to do and how you can get more of that in your next money-making venture. Remember, you're building a livelihood (streams of income that fit your lifestyle).

NEVER LET THEM SEE YOU SWEAT, IF YOU CAN.

It's okay to sweat, and it's okay to admit that you need help. But go to the people who want to help you and release your angst. When you walk into that office, show up professionally. Prepare for every meeting. Rehearse your presentations so much that you've memorized them and can deliver them without a slide if necessary. Create the slide deck, but if the power goes out, you can still do your presentation in the dark because you're not reliant on the words on the page to get you through. Never let the people looking for a reason to pick you apart see you sweat.

TAKE THE LONG DAYS AND NIGHTS UNTIL YOU'RE FREE.

While you're working on your exit strategy, there will be some long nights and early mornings when emails need to be checked and written. When you can't sleep, are you thinking of solutions? Or perhaps you dread getting out of bed to face another toxic workday. When you have an exit strategy, you can take comfort in knowing this won't be your life forever. You only need to hold on until you're able to leave for a better work situation. Take time for yourself, even if it's just a few minutes a day to do some deep breathing. No job, coworker, customer, or manager is worth your life or health. Take care of yourself while executing your strategy to escape the environment that produces long nights. Think about the life you want and the type of livelihood that can provide it.

Create long nights of opportunity. Yes, you're tired and run down, but take a vacation day or a few hours to allow yourself to explore other avenues of employment or entrepreneurship. If you know you're a writer at your core, you may need to sacrifice some sleep to write. If you want to teach, perhaps that will require you to adjunct at your local college after work. Just know that everything you do to open doors for new opportunities will be worth it. You may be tired for a while, but it's a means to an end that includes increasing your skill set so you can bring value to the next organization you join or business you start.

PROOF THAT YOU ARE INDEED THE BOMB

- They implemented your proposal after you left, AND IT WORKED! Put that on your mental resume. You have what it takes.
- They call you on the low for assistance and advice.

Whether you get credit for it or not, your implemented proposal proves that you are the bomb and that your ideas work! Make sure to take credit for it on your resume, and most importantly, remind yourself that you have what it takes. Whenever doubt sets in, revisit all the contributions you've made to your current organization to make it a better place.

If the person getting all the shine calls you for assistance and advice, you are indeed the bomb. Be careful who you share your trade secrets with, and be sure to get credit. As Maya Angelou has warned us: *You can tell what you know, but you don't have to tell ALL you know.* Keep some things for yourself. Your intellectual property is quite valuable. Make sure you are the one to profit from it.

Dream Aloud!

SIGNS YOU ARE SELLING YOURSELF SHORT

I received service awards from the department as if I were a full-time city employee. My boss raved about my performance and how I had made the company proud while playing a major role in getting their contract renewed for three more years. Then came my reward—a measly $1,000 bonus. I was disappointed but willing to show more growth to receive another raise sooner rather than later.

One day, I was delivering paperwork to the CIO's office, and he asked me to place it on his desk as he headed out to a meeting. There, in plain view, was my company's bill for services provided for the first quarter of the year. Each line item—work that I did—was more than four times my salary! I'd worked for peanuts doing the work, yet my compensation reflected the tiniest fraction of my company's revenue from the contract. It was time to move on. I had decided I wanted a master's degree and a PhD. My dream was to be a professor so I could teach what I knew while having winter, spring, and summer breaks, as well as holidays and weekends off—something I had become accustomed to while contracting with the city. My summer jobs as a teen helped me determine that I never wanted to work weekends or evenings. I wanted advanced degrees without student loan debt and began applying to local colleges and universities for my next gig.

Since I was younger, I have always taken jobs that offered me perks. In high school, I worked at McDonald's because lunch was free, at a shoe store because shoe lovers like me appreciate discounts, and at the racetrack serving gritty winners who would generously tip. I did the same in college. A children's clothing store kept my son in designer clothes for pennies, and the eye doctor I worked for provided free exams and discounted eyewear for his employees.

On President's Day 1996, I went to see Brian McKnight blocks away from the campus that I would make my home away from home for the next nineteen years. While working for the university, I took advantage of every opportunity made available to me. My first position was as a Network Operations Specialist, where I had to learn antiquated dumb terminal technology. I had come straight out of college with knowledge of the latest network operating system. Still, I quickly understood that a strong foundation and understanding of the OSI layer model is applicable no matter what technology I was dealing with.

I took advantage of every opportunity.

Please stop selling yourself short, thinking you're not good enough, and waiting for things to be perfect. People with less talent and experience are making money doing what you give away for free. Make shrinking a thing of the past when the opportunity to seize what you want comes your way. Lastly, don't assume you know what's in other people's pockets and bank accounts by telling yourself no one would pay you to do THAT!

TAKE STRATEGY-BASED ACTION

Now you know you're not alone, and your mind isn't playing tricks on you. Microaggressions are real and take a toll on your psyche and health; they can suck your soul dry. All-out social assaults can leave you so wounded that you start to believe what is said and question yourself.

We know we can only change the things we control: our own outlook, thinking, and environment. Systems do not change just

Dream Aloud!

because leadership does. Without conscious group effort to change organizational culture, the systemic engine remains the same.

Sadly, this engine changes people. Many who start out sincerely have to make choices at various points as they climb the ladder. Often, they choose promotions over activism; others decide to leave rather than stand up to the corrupt system and leadership. Those who do take a stand face punishment and retaliation and are no longer able to move up the ladder. There is such a thing as failing up, and when you see those with mediocre talent who do lackluster work continually moving up because of their congeniality or who they know, it can be disheartening. Quiet quitting is one of the results of employees realizing their hard work will never benefit them, as tap dancing and ass-kissing do in many institutions. So, they resolve to receive a paycheck until retirement. But doing just enough to slide under the radar is not what you were born to do. You have other hopes and dreams, but maybe you are unsure how to pursue them. Playing it safe has afforded you the things you want in life, but the constant worry about what's happening at work and whether you'll be the next one to get fired is no way to live. This means your job, work, and livelihood have taken over your life, and as we stated before, we want to align with lifestyle, legacy, and livelihood in that order.

Okay, enough of that. What we really want to do is get to the good part: how to use your gifts and talents to create streams of income in alignment with your purpose and passion if you are an "employed-preneur". An employed-preneur is someone who has no intention of leaving their 9-to-5 because they are close to retirement, like the benefits, or genuinely enjoy what they do. Let's get to the nitty-gritty truth.

No matter where you work, you're always going to run into the same people. They'll have different names and faces, but at the end of the day, they will be the same personalities you deal with at your current place of employment. If you are leaving your job to get away from people, I suggest you reevaluate your strategy because there will be some people you will not like and others who will not like or respect you. You must teach them to respect you by respecting yourself and your boundaries and holding fast to them.

Getting away from people is not the goal. Ultimately, your priority is to create a livelihood that is conducive to the life you want to live. Listen, it's not going to be easy, but it will be well worth it, and you can make it easier on yourself with the following principles I have gathered from my time in leadership positions.

As I mentioned before, HR is not your friend. The Human Resources Department belongs to the organization. I learned how deep this goes firsthand after I had to fire someone who was given many chances to do the right thing but failed. I worked with my supervisor and HR to follow the proper procedure to dismiss my direct report. I had completed the paperwork and an HR interview, and that was that—or so I thought. Six months later, the ex-employee applied for unemployment, which, by the way, we all pay into while working, along with welfare, Medicare, Medicaid, and Social Security. To my surprise, my organization did all it could to keep him from collecting what was rightfully his, even though he was dishonest and deserved to be fired. When you are fired, you cannot apply for unemployment for six months, whereas if you're laid off, you can immediately apply. Either way, he waited his six weeks. When he applied, not only did the organization try to stop him

Dream Aloud!

from collecting, but they also sent me with a lawyer to the unemployment office to ask them to deny his unemployment.

That was heartless, and the organization did not care. It was at that moment I realized they would step on anyone at any time to get what they wanted. When I asked the attorney who worked for them why the company wouldn't want him to have his unemployment, she replied, "Because it makes their turnover rate look bad." So, the university's statistics that the government received from unemployment were worth causing fired employees to suffer long after being penalized for the six weeks required. My employer didn't care whether the ex-employee starved or not. They didn't care that his measly $40,000 salary was absolutely nothing; it was a drop in the bucket compared to what they spent money on. To them, everything was a business deal.

Knowing this should be another reason to prioritize being the CEO of your life. Your decisions should consider your best interests first; businesses won't. At that point, I decided it would be all about my retirement plans. My department wasn't giving out raises. I later learned that the people managing budgets and telling us there wasn't enough money—placing a freeze on raises—were giving themselves raises and bonuses. That was my final deciding factor to find another space more conducive to working in peace and harmony. I took my time and began interviewing for positions, careful not to leave any clues about doing so to my staff, supervisor, or peers. While looking for a new employer that would offer the sweet spot doing what I love, which was managing projects and people while learning new technology and ways of governing projects in higher education, I began to take advantage of the health care that my current job offered in case there was a waiting period before health benefits were available at my new job. Careful to take into consideration what may not be within reach during my probationary period, I made a list of health and personal items I needed to take care of for my exit strategy and crossed them off as I completed them.

Before you begin, you first want to create your exit strategy and make sure it aligns with the next thing you want to do. Ask yourself what you can get from the job you already have before leaving. Are there certificates, certifications, or a degree you need to get that are free to you there? Make sure you don't have to stay a certain amount of time after earning the credential. If you do have to stay a certain amount of time, make sure you have the fortitude to stay or the money to buy yourself out. This means that whatever time it takes for you to get that certificate or degree, make sure you are able to stay in your position for that long, whether six weeks, six months, or a year. If you feel like you cannot get out of bed daily to go to your current job, one year may feel like an eternity.

Now, the first thing you want to do is start saving money in case you need to leave right away. If you need to quit to keep your sanity or avoid going ballistic because you're on the verge of snapping, have a stash that allows you to quit and still be able to stay afloat financially. You want to be the victor in all of this and leave the drama behind.

Knowing your company's rules is paramount for exiting victoriously. Not only should you know the organization's non-compete clause, but you should also investigate the requirements for repaying any loans you've taken from your retirement fund, as well as the rules for training and degree program reimbursement and any taxes you may be responsible for after receiving "free" education.

Some companies require employees to stay with them for a

Dream Aloud!

certain amount of time after receiving costly training. Make paying for your course a part of your exit strategy in case you need to leave your place of employment immediately. For example, if you take a course that costs $7,500 and are required to stay with your organization for two years after taking the course, your exit strategy should include a two-year plan of action. You should have a plan for all the skills you want to acquire and a list of things you want to accomplish during those two years while serving that company. Simply put, ask yourself what you can get out of them while you're still there that can help you later.

Make a plan and begin working on it. Do you need medical or dental procedures? Start taking advantage of all your company offers that will support your next steps. Is a promotion or position available that will give you leverage when applying for another position elsewhere? Take it! If you're already dissatisfied, why not get paid a little more before you leave? (Before accepting, be sure there is no 90-day grace period during which they can terminate you for any reason.) What if waiting two years to leave is not possible or worth it? Use your exit strategy savings to pay back the money as soon as you land a new gig! You can also take training as a getaway from your work environment while working to leave it. Let your current employer pay for training that you know you have set aside money to cover yourself. Use the time you're away for training as an escape from unbearable colleagues and an opportunity to network with others you'll meet during training.

Another option is to negotiate with your new employer to include paying off your training debt in your contract. Let them know you're taking training that will bring more value to your new position and that you will owe your soon-to-be former employer X amount of dollars if you leave for the opportunity they are offering. Ask if they would add the cost to some signing bonus or pay it off for you.

Try to think of every scenario that could cause an issue and create a strategy for each to make your transition as pain-free as possible. Many people just quit without a plan and then wish for their old job back when, really, they just want their old money back. Don't wing it. A properly executed exit strategy will leave you better off than you are financially and benefits-wise.

Let's go back to that list of things you do so well. Circle the things that you love to do. Remember, just because you can do something doesn't mean you should or that it aligns with your purpose and passion. Now, make a list of things you love to do that you could improve at. Also, list things you'd like to try that you've never tried before. Which of these things are you afraid to try? Which of these things do you feel cost too much for you to give a try? Which of these things are you afraid may cause other people to question your ability to make sound decisions?

We have to examine the lies that we tell ourselves. We have no idea what other people think unless they tell us, and even then, they could be telling untruths. It's not your business what other people think of you. What is your business is to figure out what you want and have enough courage to step out and go for it.

Being fearless is not a requirement to do something. You only need the courage to do it, even if you're afraid. Say to yourself, *Self, I will do it anyway.* Remind yourself that even though you're afraid of the unknown (such as interviewing for a new job or leaving the position you've held for so many years, which seems so secure), you will do it afraid, knowing that faith requires action. Have faith that the moment you decide to do something, the universe will start orchestrating things in your

Dream Aloud!

favor, ensuring that what you want becomes your reality. You don't have to believe it at the beginning. Just do it. The more you do it, the more you will believe. Remember, ACTION FIRST. Then faith builds, and then what you've hoped for becomes real.

Now, here's your assignment. You know what your talents are, what you love, and how you would like to make a living. Now the question is, do you want to be an entrepreneur or simply entrepreneurial in your work? There is no right or wrong answer here; you can also be a little of both. Another reminder for my entrepreneurs who want to step out on faith—please don't quit your day job without a plan. Create a list of goals you want to accomplish before you leave, then make a strategic plan to reach those goals. You'll be ready to leave once you hit your savings, networking, and client targets.

Before you get a coach, join a program, or spend money on anything business-related, hire a financial advisor to help you set up your business and incorporate it as they advise. This is one of the biggest mistakes people make. They put the cart before the horse. They hire coaches and marketers and have people create a logo and website but have no revenue plans. A bookkeeper is not needed until you start making sales, but you should have a tax advisor who can advise you on the type of incorporation you need for your business, and you should set up your plans for the year about how much you want to make and who you need to see next. My guess is your advisor will tell you that you need a bookkeeper or a bookkeeping practice that you can manage on your own.

As a coach, I am not against coaching, but I am against charlatans—people who call themselves coaches but have no experience in the coaching business. They are guides who will show you what they did, but they have no idea how or if it will work for you. It may have worked for certain people, but you don't need a six-figure or even a five-figure coach right out of the gate unless you are absolutely sure you are going all in. If you have all your ducks in a row, go for it. Otherwise, sit back for a moment.

Sitting back for a moment doesn't mean trying to make all the mistakes yourself. Sitting back for a moment means figuring out exactly what you want for your life and finding the coach to help you. Find someone who fits your personality, someone who will push you, someone who can see what you cannot, someone who will help you do what seems like an impossibility so you can collapse your time. Don't just pick anyone. Pick the one that's right for you.

I beg you not to use your personal money for your business. You are starting your business to add more money to your pockets, not drain them and your bank account. This is a common mistake, and I am guilty of doing it myself. When I started my business, my job was doing well, and my business was off to a good start. However, I could not get a business credit card because my business was new. So, I started using my personal credit card and good credit. Imagine if I had gone to my financial advisor to see which business credit card I should get and how I could build my business credit instead of trying to figure it out on my own. I would not have had to dig myself out of a personal debt hole I didn't have before starting my business and would still struggle to get business credit because my credit score took a dive with such a high debt-to-income ratio. Now that I can see the light at the end of the tunnel in reversing the consequences of my financial decision, I want to save anyone who will listen. Don't learn the hard way. Please seek professional financial advice for personal and business credit

Dream Aloud!

and financing from the beginning.

Hang around other business-minded people, but keep your secrets to yourself. That goes for your coach, too. There are many groups, networks, and networking opportunities, but let me tell you something: coaches are looking for new ideas, too, and they will use them, as will the people in your group. Be very careful about what you share and when you share it. Again, I am not against group coaching, but moving forward, I will make sure there is a non-disclosure agreement when I am in a group. If there isn't, I will not be in the group.

Now, let's be clear. There is no such thing as original thought. I know you want to feel like you're the only one who came up with whatever you want to do or create, but we are collectively humanity. Those of us with similar experiences will have some of the same thoughts.

"Oh, I was thinking the same thing!"

"How did they come up with my slogan? I was alone when I made it up and haven't shared it with anyone."

"Not only did I understand exactly what she meant, but I've been trying for months to find words to express what she said succinctly. What if they think I'm copying? Would that be plagiarism?"

I don't know about you, but I always want to be original. I come from the hip-hop era in which "biting" someone else's rhyme made you a thief. I now know there is nothing new under the sun, including original thought. What I think is new and original has been said, thought, and done before. But, as Brené

Brown says, it hasn't been done by me yet. I have to remind myself of this each time I hesitate to say what I want in this book, on social media, on stage, and in conversation.

I used to be afraid of being accused of stealing someone else's phrases, yet each time I spoke, it seemed like someone in my group or within earshot of me saying something would use my idea or words as their own.

Don't be afraid of being accused of stealing someone's stuff because, at the end of the day, if you actually came up with it, there will be many differences between what you have come up with and what someone else has. If you have been in a group and your coach starts speaking about things you discussed with them in private, then you have a problem. Move on. If group members begin doing things you are doing and are working as competitors, don't sweat it. Keep grinding. Keep moving forward. Keep looking for and building a support team that will help you because the idea you are actively working on cannot be duplicated. They can try, but it won't be as authentic as what you do.

As explained previously, I began working as an independent contractor while I still had my job. The first thing you want to do regarding your job is check out the employee policy. Is there a non-compete clause? If so, you may not be able to do what you do at work for your business, but if you're multi-talented, you can pick something else. If there is no non-compete clause, you are free to do what you do at work for your own business if you'd like.

My example again is that I am good at technology, project management, and teaching what I know (technology and project management) for a fee in higher ed and organizations and for free in my community. Do not balk at free because free will give you experience and exposure. You may want to rethink this when wearing your entrepreneur's hat. However, remember that promoters are most likely making money from the attendees when they ask you to speak for free at their event. They are also "gleaning" from your ideas and presentations. Whenever you decide to "donate" your time, give them the best that you've got. You never know who's watching and what doors will open.

MAKE DOING WHAT YOU LOVE SERIOUS BUSINESS

Get serious about your side hustle. When we think of what we do as just something on the side of serious work, it will always seem insignificant.

I sat at a table with influential figures and their spouses. The host of the gathering, a judge, approached the table to give me an update on the accommodations she wanted for an international tour, for which she had tasked me with providing quotes. The eyes of a judge's wife lit up. "You're a travel agent?!" she asked. "Yes, but it's just part-time," I replied, waving away any idea that I was a big-time agent who planned travel for "money is no object" clients.

Truthfully, I was good at what I did and would have been ready to serve any clients. As a member of a host agency, when I was unable to answer calls, the host agency could act on my behalf. I had conducted many group trips and tours, receiving glowing reviews for my professionalism and stellar support.

Imagine what could have been if I had treated my part-time hustle as a serious business. Consider this scenario if this had been my response when she asked me if I was a travel agent. I would have answered, *Yes, I love to travel and help others create* unique travel experiences for themselves. *Even better, I offer "Done For You" itineraries for clients who don't want to be involved in the planning.* Those influential people would have then known what I do and how I could help them. Since their colleagues trusted my services, some would have most likely purchased travel from me, too.

My full-time job had nothing to do with my growing part-time business. Why was it necessary to tell them I worked part-time in my business? My clients were satisfied and recommended me to their friends. My problem was that making an annual profit that rivaled my W-2 outside of group travel was almost impossible because I needed more high-earning clients willing to pay five figures for packages. I learned that when you decide to treat your business seriously, your outlook and income will change no matter how many hours you work in it.

Stop right now, walk to a mirror, and declare to yourself out loud, *Doing what I love is serious business.* Take it seriously, even if you consider it a part-time side hustle or occasional cash injection. Register your business, get an EIN, and open a business bank account. Tell people what you do with authority, collect testimonials, and, most of all, be the CEO who makes decisions that promote business and personal growth.

Deciding what stance you will take when opportunities arise to promote your business or convert a conversation into a sale will result in more profit and less regret about not seizing moments that will probably not present themselves again.

Now, prove to yourself that you are serious. Contact a business lawyer and a professional tax preparer to make sure you've covered your business basics. We don't know what we don't know, and ignorance can be costly. Having legal and financial guidance from qualified professionals can help you

Dream Aloud!

avoid common pitfalls that many uncounseled businesses encounter. Laws change frequently, and you want to be supported by a firm or professional who has your best interests in mind so you can focus on your business.

Too often, new entrepreneurs are courted by business coaches before they are ready. Full disclosure: I am a coach and mentor who has coaches and mentors. In hindsight, the money I've spent on coaching should not have taken precedence over securing legal counsel. I was already using my husband's CPA.

Don't just pick any professional. Look for someone who works with entrepreneurs. If you are starting or thinking about starting a business, search for legal support that focuses on new entrepreneurs. Make sure your personalities match, and, as a newbie, choose someone who takes the time to answer your questions. Most of all, they should have a genuine interest in your business and personal goals and the ability to make recommendations to meet them.

Do these things while you're still employed. Yes, some entrepreneurs think the only way to do what they do is to go all in: quit your job, not have a fallback plan, and face everything that comes your way. That works for many, but for those of us who are professionals and have grown accustomed to a certain lifestyle, we aren't willing to risk it all. Risking it all isn't necessary, but giving your all is required.

Let your 9-to-5 support you while you work on your 5-to-9. But by all means, do not bankrupt your personal funds for your business. Set a monthly amount of personal funds that you will use for the business until it begins hitting its revenue goals.

Kendra Newman

Minimal Checklist for Budding Business Owners:

- Specializes in business and welcomes new business owners
- Has readily available resources for common questions, such as FAQs, checklists, videos, etc.
- Is accessible (Clients can schedule meetings easily and get responses in a reasonable amount of time.)
- Can provide valuable recommendations
- Timely responses (You don't have to wait days for help.)
- Has automated processes and support to get quick answers when not available
- Meets with you frequently to ensure you're on track to meet your goals
- Matches or complements your personality and work with ease.
- Affordable (Relative to your ability to pay)

Hush Your Inner Critic

I've shared my stories as examples of what to do in some cases and what not to do in others. My reflections reveal how I saw myself in particular moments. Staying in a toxic work environment while being a credentialed, capable higher education technology and project management professional indicates that I saw myself as incapable of finding better employment. I saw myself as stuck at my job, but in reality, I stayed because I felt it was the best life had to offer. I let the golden handcuffs of the best health insurance I'd ever had and nineteen years of employment convince me to stay in a place for much too long.

Have you seen yourself as you truly are or how you feel you are? The goal is to have both be true. This is where we do the work to close the gap between who you think or feel you are and who you are at your core. When we acknowledge who we truly are, it becomes difficult to remain in places not meant for us.

Feeling restless in what used to feel like a place of comfort is a sign that you must do the scary thing you've been avoiding. Until you see yourself as worthy of what you desire, you will allow fear and worry to convince you to stay where you are and with what you already have. You'll never know what you're made of unless you give yourself permission to be a beginner, fail (because failure brings lessons and in no way indicates that you are a failure), and, most of all, give yourself permission to pursue your wildest dreams.

My word for the year is "discipline" AGAIN! The moment I accepted this word, its meaning and reinforcement were all around me. It isn't a coincidence; it's my focus and intention in action. I received the word two years ago and intentionally applied it daily. Reinforcement of my intention showed up in quotes and "show you better than I can tell you" examples. Then life happened, and the discipline wheels fell off. I began to ask myself, *Who are you to write a book on changing your lifestyle with a livelihood you love when you can't even find the motivation to finish?* That's the inner critic that wants to keep you from impacting the lives of the people you were born to influence.

I could hide the fact that I've encountered numerous obstacles of my own making, but I thought it was more important to share. Please know that life happens to us all! When presented with a chance to tell your story to someone who needs to be encouraged that they are not alone...do it.

In all honesty, my book was scheduled to launch in February 2023. I started writing this book six months into the new year, with "discipline" as my word and a deadline in view. At the beginning of the writing process, I was asked to take a trip to the West Coast. I intended to write during the five-hour flight each way. Instead, I slept and talked. I felt lousy on the return flight

Dream Aloud!

and tested positive for COVID-19 when I got home. My focus was on getting better; it was my first encounter with the virus, and I was tired daily! Then, my father's health began to decline, and I rightfully shifted my focus to spending time with him. He was ninety years old and told us that time was "winding up". I'd write a passage when a thought struck me and planned to pull together all the separate chapters.

Plenty happened in the year and a half that lapsed between my original submission date and now. My father started hospice treatment, and I spent every free moment with him for three months. When he passed, I thought I would be able to focus and finish my book, but we can't always control the manner in which we grieve. I'd become so undisciplined that I didn't pick a word for 2023. I saw the results of an undisciplined person—someone letting life just happen in several areas, mainly my business, book, and weight. I pretty much threw caution to the wind by the end of summer 2022 and rode that wave into 2024.

I watched my cousin posting videos as he and his family continued their pledge to eat healthier and stay fit through exercise. He ended each post with "Discipline equals freedom." I knew he was right and reminded myself that I had to be the one to make the change. That's when I decided to focus on retreat services only for my business. Yes, I still coach. In fact, I've earned another certificate, but my public-facing business consists of luxury destination retreats (and reunions) for busy hosts who want to have the freedom to enjoy their retreats as much as their attendees do. I also decided to make "discipline" my word of the year until I got it right.

I'm still trying to get it "right" as I type this manuscript. The only way I lose is if I stop trying; my discipline will not let me do that. Our shortcomings will try to hinder us when we have a goal. Don't surrender to the pressure to be perfect. The inner critic will tell you that you must be perfect to give advice, write the book, sing the song, or lead the company. Hush the critic inside with progress, integrity, and the willingness to start again when you miss the mark.

DON'T LET ANYONE ELSE PROJECT HOW THEY SEE YOU

The key words are "YOUR DREAMS". Although it was working and I got good responses, I began tweaking what I did in my new business and how I did it to fit in with the methodology of my business coaches, but it wasn't for me. I lost eighteen months of momentum trying things that didn't feel right. (I encourage everyone to try new things, explore different approaches, and take the advice of an expert, but when it doesn't work for you, fail fast, bounce back, and move on.)

Here I am, happily circled back to square one, firmly rooted in the notion that I am multi-talented. Although I have a niche in each area of my talents, I don't have to pick just one. I've given myself permission to move slowly and steadily toward the goal of my retirement lifestyle with multiple streams of income for which I only work for myself.

Outside conversations with the wrong people can give rise to your inner critic. When you try something new and struggle with it, give yourself grace. Remember that you are a beginner, so treat yourself like you would treat someone else who is a beginner. When you begin to think or say negative things about your performance, stop the thought immediately and replace it with positive words.

Stop looking externally for all of the answers. You've

Dream Aloud!

implemented solutions for yourself before, and many will work in your current situation.

Don't allow anyone else to call you into what they believe is your purpose. Take advice and adhere to the guidance you've paid to receive, but remain the CEO of your life, lifestyle, and business. Do what's best for you!

TAKE YOUR BUSINESS SERIOUSLY

This was written a few pages back, but it's so important. Most employed-preneurs fail in business because we don't take it seriously. If you treat your business like a side hustle, that is all it will ever be. You can call it whatever you want, but please operate as if it's your only source of income. This means making it a legal entity, with checking and credit accounts separate from your personal assets, and having insurance in case something goes wrong. Have a bookkeeping system and tax advisors.

Just think, if you provide a service or product that people love but only a few people know about, it will never be a lifestyle-sustaining source of income because you treat it like something you do only now and then. You have to promote yourself and toot your own horn. Let the world know you're qualified and capable of providing the best service. Until you do this, your business will never be the vehicle you need to achieve the time and spending freedom that most W-2 positions cannot offer.

Set aside dedicated time to work on your business each week. Stay committed to those hours no matter what comes your way. As a full-time employee, I have dedicated myself to working solely for my employer during organizational operating hours. I work on my business from 5 AM to 7:30 AM, Monday through Thursday, and two 4-hour nights weekly. I do not work on weekends for any entity except for engagements.

Make your business hours work for you, not keep you stuck. If you are an employed-preneur, create a lifestyle-driven livelihood instead of stuffing pieces of your life into the small, open calendar slots between jobs. Get serious about being the CEO of your life and livelihood. Remind yourself that you are also the sovereign ruler of your empire. Network with others who have been where you are going or on a similar journey so that you can go further faster than you can alone.

Beware of charlatans: the hustle coaches, mentors, and folks who tell you one thing and do another. Be careful to refrain from sharing your new ideas in circles without legal contracts to keep folks in the room (including the leaders) from stealing your ideas. They usually have more money and resources than you do and can turn an idea around faster. Protect your assets and ideas. Your intellectual property is too valuable to share with everyone. I believe some are in business to glean good ideas from people who aren't quite sure how to execute them. Just know that if they steal your idea, it's okay. Be confident that God has plenty more where that one came from. Just be sure to cover yourself the next time you decide to share. Networking, partnerships, and collaborations benefit your business when you have the proper controls in place. Don't get burned!

If You Don't Know Where You're Going, Any Road Will Get You There

You Haven't Arrived Yet!

I was supposed to meet my friend in the large parking lot at the ShopRite in Berlin to ride together to see Brian McKnight. Other friends and I waited for over forty minutes for her. She was driving from Jersey City, about an hour and a half north of our location. I gave her directions and made sure she was familiar with the area. She had been to my house many times, and I explained that she would need to drive past the street she usually turned onto to get to my house to meet us at the meeting spot. Thirty minutes in, I decided to call her, but she didn't answer.

Kendra Newman

She returned my call a few minutes later to tell me she'd been waiting in the lot for us for almost an hour.

"That's funny," I said. "We've been here almost an hour, and I don't see your car."

She began describing her surroundings, and it didn't sound familiar. So, I asked her if she had passed the street she usually took to get to my house, and she said no.

I then said, "I thought I told you to follow Route 73 south, past the Wawa on the corner of 73 and Berlin Road (the one she always took to my house) for one mile, and then turn right into the Berlin ShopRite?"

"You did," she replied. "I just felt like I'd been driving too long after I got off the turnpike, and I saw a ShopRite and waited in the parking lot."

Tired and frustrated, she declined my suggestion to meet at the venue and decided to go back home. Later, she explained everything she went through to make it to South Jersey and her defeated feeling when she realized she had wasted time in the wrong parking lot.

She was literally closer to the venue where Brian McKnight would perform than the rest of us, but she allowed a minor bout of confusion to win.

How often have you decided you've arrived and missed out on something good? What were the circumstances? If you knew what you know now, would you change your response?

Put the following list on your wall, mirror, refrigerator, or someplace you'll see it daily to remind yourself not to stop at a play that looks good because you're weary. Life has so much more to offer—if you're willing to leave your comfort zone to get what you want and other good things that you may not have been seeking.

Dream Aloud!

WAYS TO LIVE A LIFE THAT EXCEEDS YOUR DREAMS:

- Don't believe the myth of arrival. (You never really arrive.)
- When you don't know the end goal, you risk wrapping up your journey at a point that was supposed to be an experience along the way.
- Every day is an opportunity to learn something new. With new knowledge comes new opportunities.
- While you move along your journey, make good choices that will lead to multiple options that are beneficial for you.
- The wrong choices can limit your options.
- Keep your eye on the prize and know that when you reach your goal, the extraordinary now awaits. Be open to going beyond what your mind's eye can see.

There's a famous music artist who brought others along, more for his profit than theirs. No matter that he was out for himself, everyone in his sphere of influence had something to gain. He had a vision and went after it. Those who were attached to his business thought they had arrived. They had gone from the projects, food stamps, and welfare to high-end luxury condos (that they did not own), the latest high-end vehicles, and exclusive vacations. Their dream was to make an album, have the world know their name, and fill stadiums while performing on concert stages and moving the crowd. That was the extent of their dreams.

They never thought about owning homes and islands. They had more money than they'd ever seen and figured it couldn't get any better than that. They THOUGHT they had arrived.

Kendra Newman

The lead artist had bigger plans and couldn't get his protégés to see the bigger picture. He had a choice to stay where they were or move on without them. He chose the latter, while the others found themselves without shows or payment and back in their old hood on friends' couches. The entertainment world went on without them, and their lead person was unreachable.

What would life have been like for them if they had allowed the vision to grow with each goal met? Imagine the possibilities they would have envisioned if they had sought and heeded wise counsel or simply asked themselves, "What's next?" I'm sure they would have less regret and would not be wondering what could have or should have been. Do not become a part of the "Shoulda, Coulda, Woulda" club. When you reach a goal, ask yourself what's next and make a plan.

Life is a journey, not a destination. So, don't stop when you meet that first goal—you have not arrived. Actually, you will not arrive until you have taken your last breath and opened your eyes to consciousness on the other side of eternity. Please don't be the person who finds themselves on the other side of eternity regretting not taking chances. Don't have your life's work played before you and regret not going after your dream or pivoting when you find yourself on a path you don't wish to be on. There are no do-overs for many things in life, and if you don't seize the opportunity, it could leave you regretting and wondering what could have been.

NEVER LET ANYONE CALL YOU

I am a logical learner. I'm good at math and technology, and I make a living teaching others how to apply technology to their everyday lives, including their offices. In classrooms, I guide

Dream Aloud!

technology implementation to make things more effective and efficient for everyone involved. Logic and reasoning are my strong points, but I was also born a creative. My love of storytelling in any form is apparent in so many ways. I love to write, and my love for hearing the stories of others matches my passion for writing and oral delivery. I love history and weaving the past, present, and posterity together so that people understand they are the sum total of who they are, who they come from, and what they've learned. That's not all, though. I'm an excellent seamstress. I love to sew and can make things just by looking at an outfit, then go home and create it without needing a pattern.

I tell you this because, at one time, I dreamed of becoming a famous designer. I had pictures of Patrick Kelly on my bedroom wall. He was an up-and-coming designer whose shows were all the rage in Paris. It would have filled my heart to create designs of my own and see models wearing them on the runway all over the world—another opportunity to satisfy my desire to travel.

My mother explained to me that creatives don't make a lot of money and that I should stick to careers that would pay the bills. She didn't want me to struggle to pay bills as she and my dad often did. My seventh-grade math teacher said I should consider engineering because I excel at math. I'd been told even before I started school that I had a high aptitude for math. When the time came to apply for colleges, I chose engineering as a discipline. While I like math and physics even more, this did not make me an engineer at heart.

Knowing how to write and solve algebraic equations made me a standout student in physics courses. I knew how to take proper measurements and plug the numbers into algebraic equations, but I had no idea how to apply what I was doing in class to the real world. This resulted in my being on an electrical engineering path without an expected life-impacting outcome other than a college degree.

Making electrical circuits in a laboratory shocked me into the reality that electrical engineering was interesting but not something I wanted to do (at least, not in the capacity I was learning in class and labs). I wanted to work with people and see that my efforts resulted in making lives better. So, I switched to telecommunications management, studying how technology would change how we lived and worked with voice and data networking. I was excited about how this technology was being developed and loved comparing the predictions of how software and hardware would be used and how the world found uses for them. With this work, I left behind all my artistic talents and my circuit-building breadboard. Aside from the occasional request from a loved one for something I cannot find in the store for myself, I never sew.

When I was in my late 20s, I used my creative talents to paint the walls of my house with all different types of paint, sponging, and cloth, as well as to lay new flooring, sew furniture covers, and make window treatments. My projects turned out wonderful, but I never looked at them as a way to make money. I also did event planning, helping to plan weddings and decorate for events. I received many compliments, but again, I didn't feel this could be something I could do to make a great living because I let other people call me into the technology space where money and the chances of "success" were better.

Then, when the pandemic hit, I decided I would open my own coaching business, start writing books, and sell things that would help women live their dreams out loud and in color. I wanted to give them the courage to pivot from what advisors,

Dream Aloud!

family, and friends thought they should do, which brought them joy and satisfied their souls. I was doing well. People were coming to me, and I had a steady clientele. Then, I decided to get a coach to learn how to promote my book. I became addicted to coaching and felt it was what I needed to be successful. I was again letting other people call me into spaces I wasn't meant to be in, providing services that were not in line with my purpose. This led to two years of running on the hamster wheel and doing things I was told to do because I'm a rule follower.

My thought was, *They know what to do. They've done it and have been successful.* Really, all I needed to do was follow my heart and the promptings that were there. Now, I've come full circle back to what I was doing with the confidence that I should be here encouraging others and reminding them of who they are so they can tell their story and live life on purpose with passion. My work is centered around enabling others to answer their calling and undo the things that adhere to traditions rooted in slavery.

Those traditions create generalized and harmful narratives in my community. One of those things is rest. The enslaved were not permitted to rest. They worked from what was referred to as "No See To See." As the sun rose, the enslaved were already in the fields, and when the sun went down, they could finally return to their cabins. Once back home, they would work on their own gardens (if they were so blessed to have an "owner" who permitted them to do so) and tend to their children and homes before getting a little sleep to beat the sun up again for the next day of cultivating the crops.

I've been called to tell that story to acknowledge our people's resilience, fortitude, and strength and to dismantle the ill-serving beliefs we've been conditioned to praise and pass down to the next generation. When I see a Black person who always needs to hustle, be busy working, or accomplish something to feel validated, I know that they may have their reasons. For example, many may hustle because they've promised themselves that after going through a time of struggle, they never want to be broke again. Experiencing financial and food insecurity in childhood can manifest as a constant need to hustle in adulthood. Mistakes made as adults can have similar effects on individuals. These are legitimate reasons for working hard, along with phrases like "I'll sleep when I'm dead." However, the root cause is far from this. The root cause is the principle on which the U.S. was built. Based on the aristocratic system of the English crown, the British Colonies were established under the general belief that the poor were created to work the land and multiply. Idleness was considered evil. There are countless writings from early settlers complaining about lazy, low-class settlers who were unfit to live because they were uninterested in working hard. As slavery became more prevalent, the burden of work was placed on enslaved Africans, who were not permitted much rest.

There was always work to be done and children and mistresses to care for; the work never ended. Enslaved people were beaten and killed for not working hard enough or fast enough, to the point that science tells us they would go into a focused mode that compartmentalized their thinking and ability to speed up work and produce more, hoping to reduce their punishments.

The "hard work equals good Negro" narrative continues post-slavery. Many freedmen worked to build their towns and raise their livestock, only to have it taken away. The less fortunate sharecroppers did the same work they had done during enslavement under almost similar conditions. This continued

Dream Aloud!

into the Jim Crow era, where one could be found guilty of loitering, arrested, and then hired out to labor camps. So, parents have told their children from generation to generation to keep busy and stay out of trouble.

The Plantation Proverb is the reason I promote rest and leisure. During times of rest and leisure, creativity comes. Things get better when you have time to pull back and download instructions specifically for you and your life. Unfortunately, folks of little means and those of us of the melanated persuasion have never been told that it is not only okay to relax, rest, and reset, but it's a requirement to be our best. Black women have been and continue to be the poster children for hard work and also for laziness when they dare to take a break like others do. It's my mission that we now become the poster children of well-deserved rest and joy because it's our birthright.

This is something I've known from experience since my twenties. I've been a parent since I became an adult, with basically no help from my son's father. Although my parents were a great help, my mother passed away when I was twenty-two and my son was three. Add to that, mothering a high-strung ADHD boy caused me to begin taking twenty-four to seventy-two hours away for myself. During my short getaways, waking up without an itinerary or routine to follow and not having a care in the world replenished my spirit and mind. I didn't call home to check on anyone if it was under forty-eight hours.

I didn't worry about what other people thought. I did what was right for me and, in return, the best for my household. I would return rested, reset, and relaxed, which made me a better mother. Black women have been told that we need to help others and stay humble, that we don't need to be high and mighty, and that we don't need time to rest. It seems the world has decided we don't need anything from anyone. Unfortunately, we've brought this mindset into the workplace.

Being strong Black women, we work hard to be valued team members, walk the tightrope to avoid stereotypes of the angry Black woman in the office, and then go home to help family and community. But when do we make time to do for ourselves what we do for others?

I recommend everyone spend time with themselves. My preference is luxury experiences in bucket-list locations to recognize our royalty within. Luxury is self-care, and travel is transformational. Why not include traveling to a destination you've always dreamed of visiting? You can do it yourself, but honestly, allowing someone else to do it for you every now and then is great self-care. Self-care fills your cup so that you can help other people to the best of your ability. All these things are the reason I am dedicated to helping Black women acknowledge that they are worthy of the things they dream about. They are also deserving of taking time out for themselves to enjoy life. I create retreats for people to do just that. Not only do I create retreat experiences tailored to my clients' specific needs, but I also plan retreats for others to help sisters find rest on this side of the river.

My calling has led me to a position in a project management office that keeps my skills up to snuff in an environment that feeds my soul as an employee. My calling has also led me to be entrepreneurial in this space as an independent contractor in higher education, teaching project management as well as technology, and in my community with my community learning and initiative—the Each One, Teach One type of organization in which people in the community teach what they know to one another to enrich the lives of families.

Dream Aloud!

Lastly, I've created other means of income (some occasional and others passive) that will carry me into retirement so that I can live life freely and fully without the monetary restrictions of a fixed income. They include all the things I would do even if I weren't paid to do them—from my passive income in rental properties to running my planning agency, where I plan retreats and reunions. I've been doing reunions forever for free; now I have a way to continue my storytelling and coaching businesses. Through my coaching, community, and courses, I'm still helping women of color live their best lives. I truly believe that if you change a woman's life, you change the life of an entire family. I was born to encourage and will continue to do that even when I'm not paid. That's what makes my soul sing. My question to you is, what makes your soul sing? How do you find joy?

WHAT TO DO WITH JILL JOY?

You've heard the saying, "A jack of all trades, master of none." That's not what we're going for here. We're going to uncover all your skills, talents, and expertise. In figuring out your best lane, you should first know your expertise. Think of all the things you can do.

My quick example: I can plan anything from conception to realization. That's my thing. I can take your dream and help you figure out what you were born to do, then assist you in determining the best way to make it happen. It's logistics all day for me, and I have parlayed that into what I do. I'm also a master at interpreting gifts. Everything else, I only need to be good at it.

Kendra Newman

Now it's your turn to list everything you're good at doing. Don't forget to list what people ask you to do, even if you don't consider yourself an expert. Find the thing you have mastered, and if you don't have one thing you have mastered, that's where you will start mastering the thing that you love.

_____

_____

_____

_____

_____

_____

_____

_____

_____

_____

_____

_____

_____

_____

_____

_____

_____

Dream Aloud!

Once you have mastered the top thing, think of all the other things you can do to monetize your magnificence. Need help creating a plan to finance and live your dream lifestyle? You can go to kendraenewman.com to contact me. Stop allowing any road to lead you into the unknown. Set your path and follow it to a goal (or goals) you've set for yourself. If you'd like to join my group of magnificent women coming together and recognizing the gifts inside one another as we help each other reach the next level and live our dreams, visit my website for my info.

If you have been given a gift and believe it will make room for you, and you feel that something more should be happening in your life but don't know where to start, join our community. We'll be happy to have you with us. Remember, this is a journey, and it should be enjoyed. Make sure you are the navigator of your journey. It's much more impactful when you decide where you go.

Retreatment

The definition of a retreat is taking time away to rest and focus on one goal. RETREATMENT is my recipe for infusing rest into everyday life and creating extraordinary experiences that use rest as a catalyst for creativity, clarity, and courage, helping bring your dreams and goals to reality.

My business helps people experience luxury and travel at a higher level than they usually would. My niche is luxury destination retreats. Luxury is self-care, and travel is transformative.

Hustle culture has taught us to work hard, get little sleep to be successful, and sleep when we are dead. Thus, we rush from our jobs to soccer games, community meetings, and home to bed just to get up and do it all again. When do we get to enjoy the life we've been given?

The life and lifestyle-led livelihood requires a change in your thinking and priorities. To begin living the life you envision, you must change your relationship with rest. Yes, it requires hard work, but we must be as serious about rest as we are about taking action to achieve our goals.

Retreatment is a conduit for living your future life of luxury and leisure while also producing income. In the retreat, you will receive instructions on what's next. It is the place that teaches us to focus on ourselves and to fill our own cups so that we can be of better service to those we love and others for whom we provide service for payment.

You never know the value of time away for clarity until you experience it. While retreats have become all the rage, especially since the end of the pandemic, not everything labeled "retreat" meets the definition (see the first line in this chapter).

I provide support to busy professionals and organizational leaders who want to host luxury destination retreats. They offer the expertise that their attendees are looking for, and I handle the logistical planning, from location and meals to experiences that align with the host's (a.k.a. retreat leader) theme. I also offer on-site support so hosts can enjoy their retreats and ensure rave reviews and repeat business.

Family reunion hosts receive similar services because reunions are simply retreats for relatives. The difference is the standard of luxury. Because families have varying incomes and multiple members within a household unit attending, reunions must be affordable. That does not mean luxury is not an option for reunions, but affordability is a priority. My clients choose me so they can spend time with their families, enjoying precious moments instead of sitting at registration tables, handling issues, and fielding calls from loved ones and venue contacts.

I also host retreats for my coaching clients and like-minded women who need time away to focus on their new business ideas

Dream Aloud!

and care for themselves. This is where my retreat business started. My first retreat was dubbed "life-changing" by participants who raved about the experience and the level of luxury provided in a laid-back (not stuffy) style, appreciated by my clients who do not wish to be anything more than their authentic selves in all situations. The I AM Royalty Retreat is all about rest, relaxation, resetting, and reclaiming one's authority to be the CEO of her life and livelihood in a luxurious setting with service fit for an empress.

The power of rest, luxury, and travel lifts and shifts perspectives and attitudes. Attending a retreat that focuses on recharging one's batteries with these elements never gets old. I've done this for myself for the past three decades, and it's the reason I can find joy in the little things while making big plans for my future.

My retreat attendees and I travel to bucket-list destinations to see if they are places we would like to live for three to six months out of the year…or forever when we retire. Experiencing places where we'd love to work from anywhere is an added bonus to getting the rest and recharge that we need to clarify our next pivot.

Not ready for an actual four- to ten-day retreat in some exotic location? The RETREATMENT recipe will work at home or in a local hotel. Be intentional about the goal you want to achieve; sometimes, it's simply to rest and recharge. Let everyone know you'll be "off the grid" for twenty-four hours (or a few days) and that they're on their own to handle any issues that arise because you will not be available for calls, meetings, or minor emergencies.

Bring a journal and pen to write down the ideas that come to mind as you sit silently in nature or your preferred happy place.

Personal and business ideas will come to the forefront when you sit and wait in expectation. Be sure to write down what comes to mind and date them so you can review these ideas in the weeks, months, and years to come.

The best part of a review is seeing what you hoped for come to pass. Let your journal serve as your book of possibilities and proof that dreaming aloud and in color works and builds your faith muscle to face the next goal and all the challenges that come with it. You've already won when you dream big. Write it down and make a plan to stay the course. That's strategy—the plan to stay the course on the way to your goal.

Be sure to add RETREATMENT in various forms to your strategy. Many discount rest, which is why we're hearing about the "soft life" now. If you are intentional about rest, you'll never have to pivot away from hustle culture. Retreatment is a form of grace and receiving, while hustle is based on the fear of not having enough. The choice is yours. You can be a prisoner of your past fears and shortcomings or a pioneer of the life you want. May you choose the latter.

5 Keys to Live Your Dreams

START NOW

The late Myles Munroe told us that the wealthiest place on Earth is the cemetery because people with visions and dreams in their hearts, along with the skills and talents to make those dreams come true, took them to the grave instead of fulfilling their purpose. Countless men and women have passed through this life without writing the book that burned inside them, using their gifts and talents to give back to the world, or living as they wanted. Not only are the aforementioned deceased part of this "Shoulda, Coulda, Woulda" club, but there are many breathing but not truly living card-carrying members. Those who want to live life to the fullest, use every gift they are blessed with, and experience everything in their hearts' dreams must be action-takers. Only action-takers can hope they will use the gifts given to them and die satisfied to their core.

Kendra Newman

This is your invitation to spend thirty minutes each day taking action on what you want to do, see, be, or have while still breathing. I do not just instruct my clients to do this; I actually do it myself. Whenever I read a book, I take notes. If there are assignments, I complete them so that I am taking action.

Simply writing down your intention to do something new and setting a new goal in line with the "Start Now" key is a great way to kick off taking action. The successful participants in my program follow up all five key lessons with action, whether it's one-on-one coaching, group coaching, or attending a workshop. Those bound for success act early so they can ask questions during our sessions and stay after it's over to plan how best to apply what they've learned.

How does one get started in a new direction they've never been before? It's quite simple. Use what you know! Your skills and talents are transferable. Just because you've never been to Florida before doesn't mean you can't move there and be successful. You know how to drive, so you can pack your vehicle and drive it to the Sunshine State. Once you arrive, your driving skills are still necessary. The rules are roughly the same, but you have to familiarize yourself with minor nuances. *Is it legal to turn right on red? How are tolls paid here?* Now, replace moving to Florida with whatever goal you have for yourself. Is it taking a new job, starting a business, retiring, or moving to a new country? Whatever your goal, inventory the information and skills you already have, then address the gaps. What do you need to learn, or who do you need to hire to do what you cannot do?

When you are multi-talented, you must learn how to leverage your skill set to pivot and parlay what you know to assume roles that will open doors to multiple options and

Dream Aloud!

opportunities. Pivot and parlay are processes that I use in my 3L methodology. Parlay is both a noun and a verb. As a noun, parlay refers to all the skills and talents you have. If you were to think in gambling terms, it is your winnings, chips, receipts, etc.—the pile of money you've won over several games. So, think of your skills, gifts, and talents as your parlay. Now, think about what it would take to bet on you. What would it take for you to have the courage and confidence to bet on yourself? When you bet on yourself and bet big, your parlay will grow larger.

Are you ready to take on what life has to offer? You don't need another degree. You don't need more training. You don't need any additional skills to get started. If you don't act, nothing will happen. The "Shoulda, Coulda, Woulda" club awaits. Those who are full of regrets and wonder what would have happened if they had started that business, changed their brand, gone after their dreams, etc., are card-carrying members who add to the richness of the cemetery of wasted potential.

Here's my personal parlay and pivot process. I started in technology and took an interest in planning, which led me to manage technology projects for the company I worked for—my first career pivot. Within six months, I was known not only for my technology expertise but also for my professional project management skills. I turned that skill set into another stream of income as an adjunct professor at a community college. I've created a plethora of courses and curricula that I also teach. After years of teaching what I know, teaching and program creation have become highly marketable skills on my CV. I can command wages as an independent contractor for teaching, consulting, or implementing my parlay (the noun) built on the pivots I've made.

Do you see the pattern? I started something, and when I

reached my goal, I started something else. I had little experience with each start, but I did it anyway. There will always be a first time, and your expected outcome might not be so good. You can, however, rest assured that the next time you do that thing, it will be better, and you will improve with each rendition.

The Art of Start is key to fulfilling your goals and dreams. The minute you desire to do something big or new, take action right away! If you wait for perfection, you'll never do anything. Get started with what you have first, and then get better. The key is not perfection but action. Draw on your own experiences and commit to using all your gifts, ensuring that when you've reached the end of your journey, you will be content with having shared everything bestowed upon you with the world, especially with those in your sphere of influence.

This is a repeat invitation to spend thirty minutes each day acting on your aspirations. Set your intention to stay committed to working on your goals daily. The universe responds to intentional actions. Whenever the principle of reciprocity is set into motion, I urge you to observe the magic that unfolds when you articulate your desires and take tangible steps toward them.

Serendipity is a real thing, but it is not magic. It's about taking action with an end goal in mind until it actually happens. You don't have to plan how it will happen. (That's the serendipitous part.) You just need to be sure that it will indeed take place. It's when you are intentional about doing what you can and expecting that the things you cannot do "just happen" for you. Remember, we cannot do anything unless we start.

Many folks want to do something else for a living, but they don't know where to start. They're still trying to figure out what to do. I suggest researching what is required to switch to a new way of generating income so that you can live as you like.

Dream Aloud!

Notice that this first step is "Start Now." This means research is only the first step; you must take action after that. Once you know what is required, begin working to check each requirement off your list right away. Overthinking, analyzing every little detail of your plan, and doing nothing is a sure way to stay stagnant.

This Chinese proverb says, "The best time to plant a tree was twenty years ago; the second-best time to start is now." So, what would you do if you didn't start contributing to your retirement plan twenty years ago? You can lament not taking the proper steps to save decades ago or start from the day you understood you've been missing out. Then, do all you can to maximize the money-compounding opportunities available. You may not have as much in your 401(k) as the person who started twenty years ago, but you'll have something to work with, and other ventures can help you catch up. Repeat this to yourself: the best time to plant a tree was twenty years ago. The second-best time to start is now.

EMPLOY COURAGE

For four years, this key was titled "Do It Afraid". It grabs your attention. I've used this key to start my business, go live on social media for the first time, stand before crowds to speak, and do anything new that scared me. But I always knew courage is what's needed to make things happen.

Courage is not the absence of fear. It is the act of doing even though you may be afraid. The more I follow this key, the more I understand that my knees may knock and my heart pound endlessly, but I also know I've been created for this. Courage is the component necessary to get the job done.

Kendra Newman

Start Now, a.k.a. Key Number One, is easy to say, but it isn't always easy to do because fear shows up the minute you say you're going to start something new and ambitious. To make that new livelihood a reality, you've got to do something, even if you are afraid. Don't wait to be fearless. That day is probably never coming. When you wait for the absence of fear, you'll blow key number one and never start. If you know that there will be fear no matter what and that it will always try to stop you from moving forward, you'll know it's just part of the process and that it's okay to do it anyway. Knocking knees, heart pounding, sweating palms, dry mouth, stuttering—you have the power to push through it all. Courage is that power. Remember, you've got to start and then get better. So, don't worry about whether the outcome will be good the first time around. Begin, then get better as you continue.

Each time you and fear get together to talk yourself out of doing the things that will lead to the position or business you've dreamed of, DO IT ANYWAY.

When I started my coaching business, I loved what I did, but I needed to show up on social media as the authority in planning strategy to pivot into my purpose. I'm a private person. I had not done live videos and struggled to hold a one-sided conversation with an audience that would type comments about what I was saying online. I didn't want to do it. I was uncomfortable putting myself out there and having everyone see me stumble over my words. It did not work perfectly, but guess what? I did it.

The next time I did it, I felt the same, but the outcome was better. I still made mistakes, stumbled over words, and had camera problems, but some watchers commented and showed me they were interested. As I continuously showed up, I got better. It all started with my decision to begin, even though I was

Dream Aloud!

afraid. So, what are you waiting for that has kept you from starting? Chances are you're telling yourself the time isn't right, you don't have the money, or you're not good enough. Please know that none of those things can stop you from starting. We often wait for perfection. Here's a little secret: perfection does not exist. It's fear disguised as a reason to hold off on your dreams. Be courageous enough to move through fear and the unknown.

I've been researching the emotion of fear, learning what causes it and how we interpret it. Fear is a natural gift. It's a gift from God that helps us survive. Since it's part of our survival tendencies, we can also use it to our advantage in non-life-threatening situations. We must switch to courage once we realize our situation will not kill us. It's easier on our psyche and body. Courage helps us move through fear without the unnecessary feelings and pain that come with fight-or-flight adrenaline. We should save that for real life-threatening survival situations.

When fear comes, we must first decide whether our lives are at stake. If it's a life-or-death situation, you need to run, hide, or play dead. However, when it's just a fear of failure or a fear of what others will think, we need to learn to get over that hump and employ courage. Don't be afraid to let yourself down; the true letdown comes when you don't act. Not doing the thing that you know you should be working toward threatens all our dreams.

I don't believe that being fearless is necessary to accomplish any goal you have for yourself. Fear is always going to be with you. You don't need to be fearless to start. All you need is courage. Courage is the action you take when you're afraid, and it's all you need to get started. Muster up the courage to do it, say it, or whatever is required of you. Of course, we're talking about the livelihood you want in this book, but please believe that using these five keys will guide you in manifesting anything you want.

For moving forward in your heart of hearts, that dream you have for yourself will forever be a wish until you start now and employ courage. When your knees are knocking with fear, tell yourself, *I recognize that my knees are knocking.* When your heart is pounding, it's okay. When your hands get sweaty and sweat is dripping down your face, you may want to run away but stand in your power. You can do this.

Think back to the many things you've done that took courage. Now, think about where you would be if you had let fear stop you from learning to ride your bike, taking that higher-paying position, or starting your own business for more control over your schedule. With each of those accomplishments came at least one parlay and pivot move. For example, learning to ride your bike was a win in the freedom column when you and your friends could bike around the neighborhood. As you got older, you used that same skill as a low-impact exercise. Because you know how to ride a bike, you can most likely teach someone else how to ride and encourage them to get up when they fall. What would your parlays and pivots look like if you let fear stop you from getting up after a spill on your bike?

Each time you take your winnings, set your intentions to parlay your newly acquired skills and talents to make a change and pivot to better (life, pay, relationships, etc.). I would never suggest anyone do anything that I would not. Here's my story of the teaching experience that almost didn't happen.

I had sent my resume to the community college. I just wanted to teach a little technology. Instead, I built a project management program because of the parlay and pivot effect. I

Dream Aloud!

was good with that. I had a lot of fear about teaching on the first day. After that class, I got great feedback and moved on, but one of the continuing education directors saw that I had special training in an application platform that teams use to collaborate effortlessly. Most companies use it to store documents because they can't understand how it can be used outside their normal routine. It's like using a high-end vehicle that should be chauffeur-driven as a wheelbarrow. While I was allowed to "play" with the platform in my research and development space (meaning no one used it for official business), most thought it was useless, and I had no one to join me in championing it.

The platform was treasured by the community college where I worked as an adjunct. The coordinator contacted me, asking if I would teach this product to executives in partner industries—primarily hospitals and nearby casinos. Teaching was one of my pivots in a different direction. I had been moving to start bringing in some extra income for myself because I always wanted to make sure I had several income streams.

I had taken a vacation day to teach executives in their corporate education center. I created a curriculum and a guide with worksheets for attendees to follow along as I taught. I'd done it all myself, had my message down, and was ready to deliver. The night before, the judgment from within asked me, *Who do you think you are? Yeah, you know the platform, but you haven't done it at this level. You haven't taught these people before. They're all executives. They're people outside of academia, the folks you know how to teach. What if you bomb? What if it's not good? What if things don't work?*

The "what ifs" continued through the night and into the morning as I drove into the city. The only reason I didn't call and say I was sick and could not make it was that I had given my

Kendra Newman

word to them and, more importantly, to myself. I had already said I was going to do it. Wanting to put it on my résumé, I did all the work to have an impactful class.

I woke up several times in the middle of the night thinking about making sure that I did everything right, that I would have all of my handouts, that I would have everything together, and that my PowerPoint was good. That morning in the shower, I was still trying to talk myself out of this. "Am I starting to sweat?" I asked myself while getting dressed. I got in my car, and the little critical voice inside my head started challenging me, saying, *It's not too late. You could still call out. You can turn around.* These words continued to ring inside my head the entire ride. I could see the city as I drove closer, and the inner urging to turn around was undeniable. *You already have a job. What do you need this for? Why would you put yourself in such a situation? They're not paying a lot.*

I continued to drive toward the building with my heart pounding. It was a lead for me. It was a door I could open to start my income stream as a teacher and an independent contractor. This would prove that I could make a living generating income that did not come from the community college for which I was an adjunct or the university that employed me. I mustered the courage to press on. This was an opportunity to network and show people what I got so that I could do more of what I loved while not working. Thank God I didn't turn around. The Do It Courage push-through gave me the boost I needed.

The community college continuing education director met me at the door. My heart was beating, and I was shaking. It was not a good feeling. After introducing me to the HR team, the director left me to prepare for my class, which would start in

Dream Aloud!

under an hour. I went to the ladies' room several times, then set up the classroom and hoped everything would work. Twelve individuals showed up. There were six directors and their assistants. The other teams would attend weeks after the first group completed the training. I am so glad I went to that classroom and taught even though I was afraid on that first day.

My voice was a little shaky at the beginning, but ten minutes in, I was gliding through. I already knew my stuff. I just needed to show the class I did. Once I relaxed, I was able to teach the course and add impact by answering their questions with context for using the platform according to work processes and how they could adopt some features for their personal efficiency. The reviews were excellent! As I walked out to my car, I laughed at myself for wanting to quit before I even started because I was afraid of failing. I was ready to return for day two.

I could have failed, but I didn't. It's important to know that people fail all the time, and we all get a turn. Some get more than a few turns at failing. There's a lesson in that, too. You will never reap the benefits of success or the lessons from a failure unless you try.

Progress is only made when you act. Making progress will require you, on many occasions, to do things that you're afraid to do. Just remember, you're not alone. Fear threatens almost every new initiative in some way. I know that everyone has some fear and that to have life change for the better, many choose to cross that bridge to get what they want out of life. You can choose right now to summon the courage to be, see, do, and have everything you wish. I DARE YOU TO DO IT AFRAID, and with time and practice, ACT COURAGEOUSLY.

Kendra Newman

DON'T COMPARE

We've all heard it before. When we compare our success, lives, bodies, or whatever else to someone else, we rob ourselves of the ability to celebrate our progress. When we make ourselves our only competition, we celebrate each win while improving ourselves daily. Most of all, we have to lie about what we know regarding the person or situation to which we compare ourselves. To make a true comparison of how we match up against someone else, we must assume we know everything about the person and their situation. I admire plenty of people and wish to glean from their wisdom and knowledge. I've learned the hard way that I had been comparing myself to their journey and thinking I'm less than when I made assumptions about the stories of others.

What I learned: Many of the "entrepreneurs" I've admired are making six-plus figures doing what they bill as their expertise. Many of them drive Uber, affiliate themselves with products and people, sell other things on the side, and worry about how they can pay their bills.

Here I am, an employed-preneur working my 9-to-5 and running my side hustles, thinking I'm doing too much because I've been told to focus on one thing. The truth is I am multi-talented and created to make a living doing many things that I love. I am a facilitator, teacher, coach, speaker, and more. When I look closer, I see that those people who pretend to do one thing are peddling many products behind the scenes. They peddle because they have to make ends meet when flaky clients don't pay, when insurance bills are due, and when employees need to be paid. Relationships with entrepreneurs are all about money because they are the corporation. If they don't generate business, they don't have any income. There are plenty of sleepless nights, highs, and lows. If that excites you, go for it. If not, do it your way. Remember, just because they call it a side hustle doesn't mean you have to hustle unless you want to.

Next time you are tempted to compare yourself to someone else, ask yourself:

- Do I really know how they got to their position?
- Am I sure they are impeccably confident?
- Is it public knowledge that they do everything themselves?
- Have they really pulled themselves up from nothing?
- Are they really being paid X amount of dollars?
- Did they pay the full price for that item, appearance, etc.?

ENGAGE YOUR SUPPORT TEAM

Here's some advice for building your team from scratch: Don't believe what they say; watch what they do!

"Who are your seven closest friends? What are the last books they've read? Check their results. Intention without discipline is useless."

~ Caroline Myss

When you're open to help and ask for it.

Please note that you must examine the purpose of the help that arrives. Only some people will be fit for the job. Beware of counterfeits. Some will arrive for a piece of the spotlight, while others will come for a piece or all of your intellectual property to claim. Just because your cousin says he/she is rooting for you, don't believe what they say. Instead, watch what they do.

Have they consistently supported you in both success and failure in the past? Can you count on them to tell you the truth when you need to hear it, or are they just a 'yes' person? More importantly, are they a positive influence, or will they be a Debbie Downer who only points out flaws? You need to select family and friends who will provide you with the right mix of encouragement and feedback that will help you improve as you continue.

Now you're cooking with gas. Have only two or fewer of your family and friends made the cut? That's good. Now you know who you can genuinely trust. These ride-or-dies will support and defend you, your dreams, and your objectives. Knowing who you can tell your secrets and plans without having them commandeered is more than a blessing.

If you find people are unreceptive of your ideas, don't take it as a put-down. Just know they may be unable to see your vision at this time. Go ahead and live your dreams out loud, and it will be impossible for those previously unable to see your vision not to see them as they manifest.

Make sure your help is willing and able to support you in everything you do. When you find that a friend or family member cannot support you in a certain area, don't cheat yourself. Get professional support. Start with a group that specializes in the area or niche in which you want to operate. From this point, you will be able to determine if you need therapy or coaching. The one thing I have learned the hard way, and I want to save you some pain and plenty of money, is to have your bookkeeper, legal advice, and basic support in place before you seek high-end coaching. Believe me when I tell you that

Dream Aloud!

coaches need new ideas, too, and many will steal yours if you don't get the right person. Everybody who calls themselves a coach is not, and it's your job to figure out who is genuine and who is just trying to make a quick buck.

Spend some time networking. You never know who could be valuable to you in terms of providing references or support. Networking alone will shine a light on who needs your services. Tell people what you do. If you don't tell them, how will they know? Don't wait for opportunities to come to you before you tell them what you do. Go where opportunity awaits, or create your own. Attend networking sessions. Everyone is there for the same reason—to toot their horn. Show up to events and make honest conversations a way to connect with the help you need or people who need you. Being in business for yourself can get lonely, especially for the multi-talented entrepreneur who is also employed. Find spaces to meet other like-minded employed-preneurs; their company is a help.

If you don't remember anything else, remember this: Make sure your support team members are willing and capable of helping you in the areas you need.

Stay present for the process.

Every lesson you need for business and life is presented in the process. I used to be so busy working to reach the goal that I forgot to enjoy and learn from the present. Let's use reading as an example. You've been given an assignment to read the first eight chapters of a very thick book, and your professor has alluded to the fact that the contents of the chapters may appear on a pop quiz the next day or by the end of the week. Being the studious one, you know you want to begin reading right away to get an excellent grade. No matter when the pop quiz is given, you will have already read all the necessary materials.

You dive into the book and find yourself on chapter five, only to realize you've been reading to get to the end and have not comprehended a thing. Even though you read all the words, you do not understand anything the writer conveyed. So, what do you have to do now? You have to start all over again with the intention of understanding what you are reading.

You're annoyed that you've wasted time, and now you're going to go back and set yourself up for successful comprehension in a place where you can concentrate and actively take notes for later reference. When you finish this time, you know you are well-prepared for the quiz whenever it is given.

The good part about this situation is that you can start again, but there are no do-overs for some things. We're so busy trying to reach the end that we must remember to enjoy the small things. Moments instantly become memories once they have passed. When we don't take the time to pause and learn the lessons within those moments, we rob ourselves of the ability to use that knowledge for the next big thing or even for the little things.

For example, as a teen mom, I focused much of my time on the end goal rather than the process. When my son was little, I couldn't wait until he could sit up. I looked forward to when he could hold his bottle, walk, talk, and do most things for himself. I couldn't wait for him to be old enough to cut the grass and then drive himself. Then, one day, I looked up, and he was an adult.

During that time, I complained about not having support from his father and having everything on my shoulders. Paying the mortgage, car note, daycare bill, and just about everything else left me exhausted. I felt betrayed and was left holding the

Dream Aloud!

bag. I complained as often as I could. Those mature mothers of adult children would always remind me that I would make it. Although their loving, supportive adult children were living proof that I would (encouragement to keep being the best mother I could be to my son), it still felt off to me that they were so calm about it.

I am now in the season of confident middle-aged women who tell young mothers and some single fathers that they will make it and that if they stay present for the process, they will have an even more rewarding relationship with their blessings––a.k.a. their children. They, too, will learn and grow alongside their children, as I did.

I use the lessons of raising a child alone every day. I bought my first house at age twenty-seven with no help. I know what to do and how to fix things in my house because I didn't have the money to have someone else do it for me. I would go to The Home Depot and ask for "one of these and one of these," knowing it was doable. When we had no money, or it looked like we didn't have enough, it built my faith and logistical mind to figure out a way to make what seemed impossible possible. Not that it will be easy, but it won't be forever. Take time to celebrate your small wins when it feels like you're losing; most things work out well.

My biggest lesson is to have a plan and be flexible enough to pivot and change your plan to ensure you still reach your goal. You don't change the goal; you change the process. The path you start may be different from the one you end up on when you reach your goal. Some pivots were necessary. When what you thought was good turns out to be a bad idea, PIVOT. Don't let pride or ego keep you on a path that leads to something you don't want. Adjust and keep moving.

Kendra Newman

Life is for living, not for living perfectly. You start by following the promptings of your heart and making good decisions based on a plan. When the plan, or portions of it, don't work, you shift. There, you will find your resilience. Your ingenuity and creativity will keep you focused and on track when pivoting. Keep a journal because the lessons learned during a pivot are unanticipated and, therefore, unfiltered by your experiences. These lessons will be the tools you apply to your most difficult challenges.

Thank God I learned that moments are precious before my son became a teenager. Looking back on those very long days, I realize the years were short. We both worked hard, and I was tired, but it was all worth the time and effort.

I want to encourage anyone raising children or going through anything that all the lessons you need for your next chapter are right there in front of you. So, take a pause. Enjoy where you are right now, and in the moments when you cannot enjoy, ask what lessons you are supposed to learn that will help you in the future. Don't despise where you are when you find yourself in a tight spot. Don't just rush to get to the end. Stop and think: Is this a moment that will never come again? Is this an opportunity to allow your heart to teach you all you need to reach the next level in your career, become a better parent, or be a better friend? Ask yourself those questions before you hurry to get to the end.

Trust me, there will be days when you just need to get through to the end, but don't make that an everyday occurrence. Make the rush to get to the end of the day a rarity. I promise you'll be able to look back one day and say, *Oh, it wasn't that bad.*

Dream Aloud!

"Never be so focused on what you're looking for that you overlook the thing you actually find."

~ Ann Patchett

Maybe you're looking for a career change, a promotion, or a business opportunity. You'll learn more about yourself while working toward that degree, certificate, or position. What happens when you find your purpose and passion outside of the specific goals you set out to achieve? Don't overlook it; don't ignore it. Call for it, be willing to pivot, and be open to changing the outcome.

What's the difference between a goal and an outcome? Your goal for reading this book was to discover how to paint the picture of the dream lifestyle you want and the legacy you wish to live by creating a livelihood that supports it. Perhaps you thought the outcome would be working for someone else when, in reality, it's starting a new business. Or maybe you thought it was to start a new business when actually you just need to change employers or positions. In the end, all we need to do is live on purpose with passion. Who cares if it doesn't look anything like you thought it would?

One thing you thought you were looking for is the outcome. The outcomes can change, but the goal is a life, lifestyle, and livelihood that makes your heart sing and thrive. Then, leave a legacy that encourages other people to do the same. It's still the goal.

As you walk this path, don't be surprised when opportunities reveal new directions for your purpose and passion. I encourage you to stay present in the process and to be courageous enough to pivot when necessary. When this happens, know that you've found something that may not be what you were looking for but

Kendra Newman

is needed to redesign your life to match your dreams. This is exactly what happened to me. I set out to create various income streams by teaching what I know. I assumed it would always be project management and technology.

I learned that my love of history and finding the root causes of why people do things has revealed a passion for anthropology. Anything at the intersection of community, culture, and technology resonates with me. I study people's histories, the outcomes of decisions that affect them, and the effects of decision-making on their well-being.

My passion for world history, race, traditions, and behavior has led me to be more creative in my business. My creative side had been buried by well-meaning parents who did not want me to suffer financial hardships. The first half of my career in IT has afforded me the luxury of having the time to write this book, finance it, and travel while doing so. This second half is solely focused on making the world a better place through rest and leisure experiences that build and mend the hearts and minds of people. Of course, my focus is on Black women because I am one. Yet, everything I do serves anyone who understands they have a gift to give and needs to take time to cultivate those gifts so they can dispense them when prompted. My retreats are designed for busy women who want to cross off dream destinations on their bucket lists while focusing on resetting their minds, bodies, and souls to operate optimally. I've also designed family reunions, which are intergenerational retreats for related people to connect and preserve their history and traditions through storytelling.

Lastly, I continue the art of rest and leisure with my professional retreat and reunion planning services, designed for busy hosts who want to enjoy themselves at their events.

Dream Aloud!

I affirm that you are worthy of having the lifestyle and livelihood of your dreams that will leave a legacy you are proud of because you've dared to DREAM ALOUD!

May you do the work that brings you full circle to be the person God intended. May you live fully on purpose with passion. May you use your talents to the fullest and have few regrets. May you dream aloud and in living color!

About The Author

Kendra Newman, PMP, is a Project Management and Strategy Planning professional with 25+ years of experience shepherding higher education leaders through information and technology integration and innovation. As the founder of Kendra E. Newman Planning Strategies and Chief Learning Officer of an elite retreat concierge training academy, she plans, hosts, and manages the production of luxury destination retreats for busy coaches, experts, and organizations who want to create additional revenue streams in their business.

A master experiential facilitator, Kendra also hosts retreats and workshops to teach black women to leverage the sum total of their experience to create multiple streams of income doing what they love to DREAM ALOUD and LIVE IN COLOR!

Most of all, she's living her life with the courage to be the planner, writer, and speaker she was created to be. She reminds others of the importance of REST so that we can be fully present when it counts.

You can learn more about Author Kendra E. Newman's planning strategies, elite concierge academy, retreat and reunion planning, or any of her processes for living and working as you've dreamed at connectwithkendra.com.